USAF SPECIAL AIR WARFARE

DOCTRINES AND CAPABILITIES, 1963

(U)

By
Charles H. Hildreth

August 1964
USAF Historical Division Liaison Office

FOREWORD

This study continues through 1963 the account of Air Force special air warfare activities begun in AFCHO study <u>USAF Counterinsurgency Doctrines and Capabilities--1961-1962</u>. (The broader term--special air warfare--replaced the term counterinsurgency in the Air Force late in 1963.) In the current study the author recounts the continuing Air Force-Army struggle over special warfare roles and missions; the OSD acceptance of an Air Force proposal to increase its special air warfare force; the Army's efforts to add organic aviation to its Special Forces; the relationship of STRICOM to the special warfare forces of the services; the buildup of special air warfare units in the unified commands; the growing importance of civic action and mobile training teams in underdeveloped nations; and progress in securing more modern aircraft.

Although this study forms a part of a larger <u>History of Headquarters USAF</u>, it is being published separately to make it more readily available.

JOSEPH W. ANGELL, JR.
Chief, USAF Historical Division
    Liaison Office

CONTENTS

I. Special Air Warfare Planning and Controversy.......... 1
    USAF PCP-3................................... 7
    The Army PCP................................. 12
    Relationship of U.S. Strike Command to Special
        Warfare Forces............................. 16

II. Expanding Special Air Warfare Capabilities............ 28
    Buildup of Units................................ 29
        SAWC Reorganization........................ 29
        PACAF...................................... 29
        USAFE...................................... 35
        CAIRC/USAFSO............................... 38
    Civic Actions................................... 39
    Mobile Training Teams........................... 44
    Search for Improved Special Air Warfare Aircraft... 50

NOTES... 57

GLOSSARY.. 64

I. SPECIAL AIR WARFARE PLANNING AND CONTROVERSY

Through the 1950's the United States considered general war the primary military threat. Although the armed forces recognized the danger of subversive insurgency in underdeveloped areas of the world, the subject received considerably less attention than the threat of general or limited war in the U.S. basic security policy. As late as January 1961, when Khrushchev made his famous "wars of liberation" speech, the United States possessed no forces specifically trained in counterinsurgency operations. Army Special Forces were organized to conduct guerrilla warfare--but only in support of conventional military operations. The Navy and Air Force had no units specifically designed to combat insurgency. However, it was generally assumed that a latent capability existed within the military forces to meet many of the tasks required in a counterinsurgency effort.

With the advent of the Kennedy administration in January 1961, the situation changed. The new President directed the Joint Chiefs of Staff (JCS) to examine "the troop basis of U.S. armed forces to insure an adequate capability in all types of units required in counterguerrilla operations, or in rendering training assistance to other countries." As a result of this review, the Air Staff recognized the need for a small specially equipped force of highly trained personnel to serve as a nucleus for the USAF contribution to the counterinsurgency mission in cold war and the unconventional warfare mission in hot war.*

---

*For more details on activities preceding 1963, see Charles H. Hildreth, USAF Counterinsurgency Doctrines and Capabilities, 1961-1962 (AFCHO, Feb 64).

In mid-April 1961 the Air Force activated the 4400th Combat Crew Training Squadron--Jungle Jim--at Hurlburt Field, Fla. Initially, the squadron consisted of 16 C-47's, 8 RB-26's, and 8 T-28's. By 1 July the unit was fully manned--125 officers and 235 airmen. Its mission consisted primarily of preparing small cadres for conducting--at the scene of insurgency activity--the training of friendly foreign air forces in counterinsurgency operations, as well as participating in them if required. The unit also worked closely with the Army Special Warfare Center at Fort Bragg, N.C., in counterinsurgency and unconventional warfare training. In September 1961 the 4400th became operationally ready and almost immediately began preparations to send a detachment to South Vietnam (SVN). In November this detachment (Farmgate)--composed of 4 C-47's, 4 RB-26's, 8 T-28's, and 151 personnel--moved into Vietnam to train the Vietnam Air Force (VNAF) for operations against the Communist-supported Viet Cong and to participate in operational missions beyond the capabilities of the VNAF. On such missions, a combined US-SVN crew was required.

Since this initial detachment took almost half of the USAF resources specifically trained for counterinsurgency, the Air Staff decided in December 1961 to double the size of the squadron and make it a group. Shortly after this decision, on 11 January 1962, the President registered his discontent with the efforts of the Department of Defense in meeting the subversive insurgency threat and directed that it take corrective action. In response, the Air Force assessed the anticipated air requirements of the unified commanders and the requirement to insure adequate air support for the expanding Army Special Forces, determining that it needed a force of approximately 250 aircraft and 5,700 personnel. Then it submitted a

Program Change Proposal (PCP-1) reflecting this need to the Office of the Secretary of Defense (OSD) in May 1962. At the same time it activated the Special Air Warfare Center (SAWC), expanded the 4400th CCTS into the 1st Air Commando Group, and established the 1st Combat Applications Group.

As the Air Force was the first to submit a PCP for expanding counterinsurgency forces, OSD delayed its decision and requested the other services to submit their proposals. The divergent views on counterinsurgency air operations held by the Army and the Air Force became openly apparent both in the PCP's they submitted and in the comments each provided on the other's proposal. These divergencies were directly related to the issue of roles and missions--specifically, who would supply and control the aviation tailored to special warfare operations.*

The Army maintained that its organic aviation--designed to enhance its tactical mobility--was best suited for the task because "low performance" characteristics permitted it to operate in a primitive ground environment and allowed greater target selectivity. The Army buttressed this argument with the premise that flying personnel should identify themselves with the ground personnel they supported and that this identity was best

---

*Special warfare included counterinsurgency and unconventional operations. JCS definitions beginning July 1962:
    Counterinsurgency--Those military, paramilitary, political, economic, psychological, and civic actions taken by a government to defeat subversive insurgency.
    Psychological warfare--The planned use of propaganda and other psychological actions having the primary purpose of influencing the opinions, emotions, attitudes, and behavior of hostile foreign groups in such a way as to support the achievement of national objectives.
    Unconventional warfare--Includes the three interrelated fields of guerrilla warfare, evasion and escape, and subversion. Unconventional warfare operations are conducted within enemy or enemy-controlled territory by predominantly indigenous personnel, usually supported and directed in varying degrees by an external source. (JCS Pub 1, Ch 1, 2 Jul 62.)

achieved by being a part of the same unit.

The Air Force adhered to the doctrine that aircraft should be centrally managed under the operational control of a qualified air officer. Centralized management with decentralized operations, the Air Force argued, permitted concentration of air support where it was most effective. Responsiveness to the needs of the ground troops would be achieved by using forward air controllers assigned to the ground units.

In essence, the Air Force believed that the Army was seeking unilateral control of the entire special warfare function by attempting to control air support as well as ground operations. The Air Force insisted that special warfare should be a joint undertaking with each service doing those missions that it was best able to perform. Air support--a basic aviation function--could best be performed by the Air Force.

OSD acted on the Air Force and Army PCP's in August 1962. It disapproved the USAF proposal and directed the Air Force not to expand its counterinsurgency forces without prior approval. At the same time, OSD rejected the aviation portion of the Army PCP.

The restriction on the size of the Air Force's counterinsurgency forces came during a period of increased demand. Requirements in Southeast Asia and Latin America continued to grow, and in October the Air Force submitted PCP-2. The Army again opposed this programmed expansion, essentially for the reasons previously voiced. However, the new USAF proposal, calling for a force of 184 aircraft and 2,167 personnel (6 squadrons) in fiscal year 1964, won the support of CINCARIB and CINCPAC, and OSD approved it on 24 November 1962. The Secretary of Defense requested that the Air Force attain the objectives as soon as possible within the constraints of fiscal year 1963 manpower and budgetary limitations.[1]

The basic principles governing U.S. military participation in special warfare operations were set forth in Unified Action Armed Forces (UNAAF--JCS Pub 2) and in the Joint Counterinsurgency Concept and Doctrinal Guidance (JCS Memo 1289-62). Appropriate annexes to the Joint Strategic Capabilities Plan (JSCP), the Joint Strategic Objectives Plan (JSOP), and in statements of high government officials provided specific guidance. The central theme of this guidance was that special warfare operations should be joint undertakings involving all military services.[2]

The Air Force emphasized this joint approach throughout 1963, beginning with the issuance of its long-range cold war objectives in January. It listed as a major objective the defeat of Communist insurgency movements by (1) organizing, equipping, and providing air forces for counterinsurgency operations and for support of country programs; (2) developing, in coordination with the other services, the doctrine, tactics, procedures, and equipment employed by air forces in counterinsurgency operations; and (3) participating with the other services in joint training and exercises.[3]

A year later, the Air Force Chief of Staff, Gen. Curtis E. LeMay, in testimony before a congressional committee, pointed out that experience gained during the past several years proved the Air Force's unique capability to contribute in the field of special warfare. He stipulated: "This capability should be closely aligned with that of the other Services to prevent duplication and waste of our national resources. The joint employment of these specifically trained and equipped units under a centralized control is the most effective and economical means of meeting our commitments."[4]

The controversy between the Army and the Air Force over roles and missions--specifically, whether there should be joint or unilateral control of special warfare--continued through 1963. It was evidenced in nearly every discussion within JCS concerning the buildup, operational control, and use of special warfare forces. This was especially noticeable in the discussions of the JSOP for 1968, Air Force PCP-3, and Army PCP and in the relationship between the individual services and the U.S. Strike Command (STRICOM).

The JSOP, the primary document used by JCS in providing guidance to the military services on force structures, covered a five-year period. From it, the services obtained support in justifying and preparing their annual budgets, and it served as a point of departure for developing future requirements. JSOP-67, approved by JCS in August 1962, established a USAF counterinsurgency force objective of 10 squadrons, and the three service chiefs noted their accord. However, when JCS considered JSOP-68 in the spring of 1963 the Army Chief of Staff opposed any increase in the number of units beyond the six squadrons approved for 1964 on 24 November 1962. The Navy took a compromise position that favored eight squadrons. The Air Force insisted on 10, maintaining that it needed this minimum number of squadrons to meet commitments levied by the unified commands and the Army's training program. Only a 10-squadron force could provide a nucleus of highly trained personnel capable of dealing with the threat posed by the Communist Bloc throughout the world. When JCS could not resolve the question, it forwarded split views in April 1963 to Secretary of Defense Robert McNamara.*5

---

*Secretary McNamara made no formal reply but his decision in favor of the 10 squadrons was inherent in his approval of PCP-3 on 30 October 1962. (See below,

USAF PCP-3

The question of USAF special warfare expansion became even more acute with JCS consideration of the Air Force's third Program Change Proposal (PCP-3). In accordance with Secretary McNamara's instructions, during the first half of 1963 the Air Force was building from within its own resources to meet the approved force of six squadrons. However, it knew that even after attaining this goal it would lack sufficient forces to meet known theater operational requirements and still retain an adequate force in the United States for training and unforeseen contingencies. Stated fiscal year 1964 requirements of three unified commanders--concurred in by JCS--demanded the oversea deployment of 107 of the 184 aircraft in the 6-squadron program, and additional requirements were expected. At this rate, about 82 percent of authorized transport aircraft and 44 percent of strike/reconnaissance aircraft would be overseas at all times, leaving insufficient flexibility for other operations.[6]

During May and June 1963 the Air Force prepared and coordinated through its Air Staff Board a PCP designed to meet minimum special air warfare requirements; on 18 July it submitted this PCP to OSD. The paper proposed to change the name of the forces from counterinsurgency to special air warfare (SAW)--a name more in line with their expanding missions--and called for an increase in the SAW structure from 6 squadrons with 184 aircraft and 4,457 personnel* to 10 squadrons with 253 aircraft and 6,365 personnel in fiscal years 1965-66. Personnel strength would decline to 5,948 for

---

*In the May 1963 updating of the DOD Five Year Force Structure and Financial Program, direct support personnel were included in the primary element, and the SAW force personnel figure was raised from 2,167 to 4,457. (Background Paper on USAF SAW PCP, prep by D/Plans, nd, in SW Div files.)

the following two years. The net increase over the five-year period would total 69 aircraft and 1,491 personnel.[7]

By June 1963 the requirements of the unified commanders far exceeded the capabilities of the programmed six-squadron force. Four of the commanders--CINCLANT, CINCPAC, CINCNELM, and CINCEUR--included their SAW requirements in JCS-approved war plans. For example, the CINCLANT plan for contingency operations in Africa south of the Sahara (Oplan 330-63) required a SAW detachment of 24 aircraft and 150 personnel for each of 9 Army Special Forces companies committed. The CINCLANT plan for Cuba (Oplan 312-63) stated a general requirement for a SAW force for unconventional warfare. In the Pacific, CINCPAC's general war plan (Oplan 1-63) required unconventional warfare airlift, and his plans for the defense of Korea (Oplan 27-63) and defense of the mainland of Southeast Asia (Oplan 32-63) required three SAW detachments to provide airlift, strike, forward air control, and reconnaissance support in Korea, Vietnam, and Thailand or Laos. CINCPAC did not specify explicitly the SAW requirement for the defense of Taiwan/Penghus (Oplan 25-63), stating only a general need for airlift, strike, reconnaissance, etc. In the Middle East, CINCNELM (Oplan 200-63) wanted the Air Force to furnish airlift for infiltration, exfiltration, and resupply. On 11 June 1963 CINCEUR requested JCS to approve a SAW unit in Europe composed of 16 aircraft and 150 to 180 personnel to handle tasks in both unconventional warfare and counterinsurgency during fiscal year 1964. He also emphasized a need for joint counterinsurgency mobile training teams (MTT's) and for Air Force units to work with the Army's 10th Special Forces Group.[8]

By May 1963 the Air Force had deployed about 80 aircraft in support of the special warfare effort in South Vietnam alone, including TAC's two C-123 squadrons (Mule Train/Saw Buck)* and the Farmgate detachment. In addition, the SVN government intended to implement a national plan that would increase combat airlift requirements significantly, and this would have to be met by C-123 aircraft. At the same time, a composite squadron (Bold Venture) from the 1st Air Commando Group was in Panama with 14 aircraft and 96 personnel to provide CINCARIB with a special air warfare capability, and plans were under way to increase its size to 46 aircraft and 545 personnel before the end of fiscal year 1964. The Vietnam and Latin American requirements alone would leave the U.S.-based SAW force so depleted as to preclude adequate and timely response to other global requirements and unforseen contingencies.[9]

The rapidly growing Army Special Forces--expected to number 9,060 by 30 June 1964--required increasing numbers of SAW units to furnish air support. In addition, SAW forces participated in joint unconventional warfare exercises conducted by STRICOM. Finally, SAW units in the United States served as replacement and training centers for the deployed units.[10]

Since the greatest shortage was in the area of airlift, the Air Force in PCP-3 had proposed that 75 C-123's be added to the SAW force and that 2 C-47's and 4 T-28's be deleted from it, resulting in a net increase of 69 aircraft. Forty-four of these additional C-123's would serve in PACOM, 16 in EUCOM, and 15 in the United States.[11]

To meet the overall needs of the unified commanders, the Air Force determined that 3 composite squadrons with 84 aircraft should be deployed

---

*See Hildreth, p 47.

in PACOM, 1 composite squadron of 46 aircraft in CARIBCOM, and 1 composite squadron with 30 aircraft in EUCOM. Five reduced squadrons (3 strike/reconnaissance, 1 troop carrier, and 1 utility) with a total of 93 aircraft should remain in the United States to train with both Army Special Forces and STRICOM and provide a capability to meet contingencies or augment other oversea forces. The U.S.-based units would provide replacement training and MTT's. Approval of PCP-3 would allow growth to this overall capability by the end of fiscal year 1965 at an increased cost of $9.7 million for fiscal year 1964, $18.4 million for fiscal year 1965, and $83 million for the 1964-68 five-year period.[12]

Late in July the Joint Staff discussed PCP-3 and agreed that global requirements for special warfare forces had expanded rapidly and would continue to increase. The Navy, which had recommended only 8 SAW squadrons in JSOP-68, indicated recognition of the need for increasing the Air Force's special war capabilities to the 10-squadron level. The Army opposed any further increase, reaffirming the position taken on JSOP-68 that 184 SAW aircraft were sufficient to meet requirements in current operational plans. Increased transport needs could be met by assigned theater airlift, with the C-123's remaining in the general purpose airlift force.[13]

Disagreeing with the Army position, the Air Force pointed out that the force of 107 airplanes currently required by the unified commands was based on fiscal year 1964 plans and would inevitably increase. While it was true that many contingency plans did not state numbers of aircraft required, they did show the need for SAW units in the event of trouble, and it was essential that these units be available.

With regard to airlift, the Air Force agreed that general purpose airlift could augment SAW forces, but command and control would be extremely difficult. Special warfare operations would normally include long periods of TDY for U.S.-based air transport forces. Moreover, since the areas of deployment for special warfare airlift--Latin America, Middle East, Africa, Southeast Asia--were usually far removed from general purpose airlift bases or routes, SAW airlift units should operate under theater or unified command control. The Air Force also noted that airlift units assigned to Vietnam operations would not only perform special warfare tasks but also some of the troop carrier tasks normally handled by general purpose airlift forces.[14]

On 30 July 1963 JCS took PCP-3 under formal consideration. After the Air Force and Army chiefs of staff were unable to compromise their differences, JCS forwarded divergent views to OSD on 1 August. On 30 October Secretary McNamara approved PCP-3, thus authorizing the transfer of the 75 C-123's, approving the additional manpower and budgetary requirements for fiscal year 1965, and changing the designation of these forces from counterinsurgency to special air warfare. The following tables show the extent of the increase:[15]

Funding (In Millions)

	FY 64	FY 65	FY 66	FY 67	FY 68	Total
Previously approved	35.9	34.5	34.5	34.2	34.2	
PCP-3	45.6	52.9	55.0	51.9	50.8	
Increase	9.7	18.4	20.5	17.7	16.6	83.0

Manpower Authorizations

	FY 64	FY 65	FY 66	FY 67	FY 68
Previously authorized	4,457	4,457	4,457	4,457	4,457
PCP-3		6,365	6,365	5,948	5,948
Increase		1,908	1,908	1,491	1,491

Approved Aircraft Levels

Type	FY 64	FY 65-68	Change
B-26	33	33	0
T-28	33	29	-4
A-1E	50	50	0
C-46	24	24	0
C-47	18	16	-2
HC-47	6	6	0
U-10	20	20	0
C-123	0	75	+75
Total	184	253	+69

The Army PCP

The Army's attempt to expand its special warfare aviation strength began in 1962 with the submission of a PCP that in part called for a special warfare aviation brigade headquarters and five aviation squadrons. The mission of the headquarters was nearly identical to USAF's Special Air Warfare Center (SAWC). Its squadrons designated for Southeast Asia and Latin America duplicated the Farmgate and Bold Venture units, and the squadrons slated for Africa and the Middle East were comparable to the Air Force units planned for those areas in PCP-3. It appeared that the Army's U.S.-based special warfare aviation squadron would duplicate the existing capabilities of the 1st Air Commando Group. The Secretary of Defense rejected the aviation portion of the Army PCP in toto on 27 August.[*16]

The Army then turned to other means of obtaining special warfare aviation--budget addendums and revisions to unit tables of organization and equipment (TO&E). On 27 September 1962 the Army in a budget addendum for fiscal year 1964 asked OSD to authorize 12,987 personnel spaces for its special warfare forces, an increase of 3,920 spaces at an additional

---

*See above, pp 3-4.

cost of $26,379,720. Secretary McNamara gave partial approval on 4 December, allowing expansion to the degree that the Army could man and finance it within its fiscal year 1964 resources.[17]

Accordingly, on 16 August 1963 the Army submitted a PCP to OSD calling for 2,529 additional personnel in its special warfare forces during fiscal year 1964--the increase and financing to come from current resources. These personnel would man a new Special Forces group and augment three existing groups based in the United States and would provide specially trained, area-oriented forces for Southeast Asia, Latin America, Europe, the Middle East, and Africa. There was no indication what portion of these expanded forces would be used for aviation. Although informally acknowledging that part of the increase would supplement Special Forces aviation strength, the Army insisted that it was impossible to identify the amount. Furthermore, such identification in the PCP was unnecessary under the Army system of bolstering its aviation elements by unit TO&E revisions.[18]

The Army claimed it had the authority to introduce aviation into its units in this manner. In a lecture given at the Army Special Warfare Center, an Army spokesman said:

> The air has become an additional element in which the Army operates. Aircraft have greatly increased battlefield mobility by eliminating the obstacles imposed by mountains, jungles, swamps, and bodies of water. Aircraft for this function remain a part of the ground environment and contribute directly to the local ground operations. Such aircraft are merely vehicles which discharge Army functions more effectively than can be done by ground vehicles.

In essence, the Army maintained that it possessed the right to assign aircraft to its units in the same fashion as tanks, trucks, or artillery. On 8 August 1963 Secretary of the Army Cyrus R. Vance, in defending this practice, informed Secretary McNamara that he interpreted the 27 August 1962 decision as a specific disapproval of a special warfare aviation brigade and not a general prohibition of Army special warfare aviation. McNamara did not reply to this statement, thus giving at least tacit approval to the Army practice.[19]

The Air Force was gravely concerned over these Army tactics for a number of reasons. It deemed the addition of aircraft to an organizational unit as a significant change in resources, force composition, and combat capability. Consequently, JCS should consider such changes. More to the point, the Air Force realized that Army aircraft were capable of reconnaissance, strike, transport, and utility uses, and once the Army Special Forces possessed sufficient organic aviation they could be expected to call on the Air Force for only that support beyond Army aviation capabilities. Likewise, the Air Force felt that JCS should have had the opportunity to consider the Army 1964 budget addendum prior to its submission to OSD. This authorized expansion--even though the personnel were a part of the previously approved overall Army force structure--added to the Army Special Forces at the expense of other combat units. In short, the Air Force argued that the Army was subverting the intent and purpose of the PCP system through its efforts to increase aviation strength in the special warfare area.[20]

In the JCS discussions on the PCP, the Air Force objected to the Army's "inability" to identify the aviation elements in the proposed expansion. The Air Force did not oppose the increase in Army special warfare ground forces but was strongly against an expansion of aviation strength, and therefore it could not recommend approval of the 2,529 additional spaces when it did not know the job or purpose of these men. General LeMay also pointed out that the Joint Staff was currently engaged in a study to determine proper Army and Air Force roles and missions for all aircraft and that a decision on the Army PCP should await the results of that study.*21

JCS reached a split decision on 4 September 1963. The Chairman, the Army Chief of Staff, and the Chief of Naval Operations considered the PCP responsive to military requirements and recommended approval. While noting that the Army would utilize an unspecified portion of the funds and manpower spaces to support aviation units organic to its Special Forces, they stated that pending the results of the Joint Staff review it was inappropriate to consider the matter of aviation support for these forces. The Air Force Chief of Staff could not see the logic of this argument. He failed to understand how JCS could recognize the existence of aviation in the PCP, approve its content--indirectly approving the aviation element-- and at the same time state that it was inappropriate to consider the matter of aviation support. Therefore, the Air Force recommended that PCP approval be limited specifically to expansion of ground forces with no funds or personnel authorized for aviation support until after the review of roles and missions. JCS sent these views to OSD on 17 September.22

Secretary McNamara approved the Army PCP on 29 October 1963. In so

---

*On 19 June 1963 JCS had directed J-5 to organize a study group to consider the responsibilities of Army and Air Force for all uses of aerial vehicles and to recommend revisions to appropriate directives. The Joint Staff prepared a study based on service inputs and J-5 deliberations. (JCS 1478/99, 19 Sep 63.) The disagreement between the Army and Air Force was so deep that the Operations Deputies of the JCS could not agree on a statement of the basic issues. (DSAFM 627-63, 9 Oct 63.) After a number of unsuccessful meetings of the Deputies, JCS agreed that the two chiefs of staff would attempt to resolve the differences. Although a number of meetings were held, they achieved no substantial results. As of 30 December 1963 the controversy over service functions remained unresolved. (Hist, D/Plans, Jul-Dec 63, pp 313-15.)

doing, he stated that his decision was not to be interpreted or implemented in a manner prejudicing the review of the roles and missions of either the Army or the Air Force with respect to aircraft. He limited Army Special Forces aircraft and aviation personnel to the number scheduled in the DOD Five Year Force Structure and Financial Program, as revised by the PCP. The last clause, "as revised by the PCP," was important since an indefinite amount of organic aviation was included in the PCP. Although qualified, this decision allowed Army aviation for the Special Forces.[23]

Secretary Zuckert firmly reiterated Air Force arguments to Secretary McNamara on 12 December. He asked for a reappraisal and modification of the decision so that the Army would not commit organic aviation resources to Army Special Forces until JCS completed its current review of roles and missions. Early in 1964 the Secretary of Defense replied that he had reviewed his decision and saw no reason to change it.[24]

Relationship of U.S. Strike Command to Special Warfare Forces

Several skirmishes over roles and missions took place during 1963 between the Army and the Air Force in determining the relationship of the services to STRICOM. A variety of issues were involved: collocating Army and Air Force special warfare centers; assigning to STRICOM operational control of U.S.-based combat-ready special warfare forces; and planning and after-action discussions of Swift Strike III. In general, the Air Force cooperated fully with the desires of STRICOM since CINCSTRIKE's ideas generally paralleled those of the Air Force on joint control and planning of special warfare operations. The Army, in support of its interest in securing unilateral control of special warfare activities, usually opposed CINCSTRIKE recommendations.

In September 1962 CINCSTRIKE had suggested establishing a Joint Special Warfare Coordinating Group (JSWCG) under STRICOM. JCS agreed and forwarded its recommendations to OSD. On 6 December Deputy Secretary of Defense Roswell Gilpatric approved the proposal and requested the group to make a detailed study of the advantages and disadvantages of collocating the Army Special Warfare Center and the Air Force Special Air Warfare Center.[25]

On 14 January 1963 CINCSTRIKE forwarded the JSWCG report and his own recommendations to JCS. JSWCG had been unable to arrive at a definite decision. CINCSTRIKE, while recognizing certain advantages in collocation, recommended against the move because he felt the cost would outweigh any benefits. However, he reintroduced the suggestion made in 1962 that STRICOM should possess operational control of combat-ready special warfare units based in the United States. JCS's Special Assistant for Counterinsurgency and Special Activities (SACSA)--in collaboration with J-5--studied the problem and agreed with CINCSTRIKE.[26]

During the closing days of January, JCS discussed the issues and agreed that CINCSTRIKE's recommendation against collocation was correct. It also agreed on the need for more effective development and coordination of special warfare doctrine, tactics, techniques, and equipment and recognized that STRICOM should play a major part in this area. That this need could best be met by granting STRICOM operational control of U.S.-based special warfare units was a matter of contention.[27]

The Army believed that special warfare forces of both the Army and Air Force should be made available to STRICOM to the "maximum extent possible" for joint training exercises and to develop doctrinal recommendations for JCS. As the buildup of special forces continued, the Army stated, increased numbers could and would be made available to STRICOM. Currently, however, it was unable to furnish additional forces to STRICOM. In taking this position the Army noted that the bulk of U.S.-based special warfare forces were or would soon go overseas to satisfy operational requirements and that the remainder were supporting the Army Special Warfare Center and School, training Army special warfare backup brigades, and participating in joint training exercises of unified commands--including STRICOM. Finally, the Army felt that granting STRICOM overall cognizance for special warfare would conflict with assigned responsibilities of the services and unified commands. The Navy supported the Army position.[28]

The Air Force argued that more effective coordination on doctrine, tactics, techniques, and equipment could best be accomplished by assigning operational control of special warfare forces to STRICOM as they became combat ready. Making forces available for joint training exercises merely maintained the status quo that had proved inadequate. Moreover, the Air Force maintained, benefits could be expected in special warfare similar to those resulting from assignment of other tactical forces to STRICOM.[29]

JCS was unable to agree and on 30 January 1963 decided to forward split views to OSD. The Chairman sent the divergent positions, reserving his own until he could give the matter further consideration. On 13 February he informed OSD of his agreement with the recommendation against collocation and, because of the shortage of U.S.-based combat-ready special warfare forces, recommended that no units be assigned to STRICOM's operational control in the _immediate future_. He did not close the door to STRICOM operational control at a later date. Recognizing that the divergency of opinion between the Army and the Air Force was "an outcropping of the more basic issue of the proper responsibilities of the Services and of STRICOM in the field of special warfare," he directed the Joint Staff to look deeper into the basic issue and informed OSD that he would offer further recommendations before 1 April 1963.[30]

On 19 March the Joint Staff reported the conclusions of its investigation. It emphasized the need for joint training and the development of joint doctrine, tactics, techniques, and equipment for those special forces JCS might direct STRICOM to employ. It also recommended operational assignment to STRICOM of an initial working force of an Army Special Forces company and a composite psychological warfare detachment as soon as they were available. In addition to the USAF medium and assault troop carrier units already assigned, STRICOM should assume operational control of one 1st Air Commando Group composite squadron.[31]

The Air Force supported the Joint Staff recommendations as one step, albeit a small one, toward improving joint special warfare doctrines and operations. This was a compromise of its 30 January position that all U.S.-based combat-ready special warfare forces should be assigned to STRICOM and was the maximum compromise the Air Force could accept without completely abandoning this earlier position.[32]

The Army nonconcurred with the Joint Staff recommendations. It opposed assignment of operational control now or in the future, contending that any requirements for joint training exercises could be met by making forces available to STRICOM on a temporary basis. As in the past, it appeared that the Army desired to retain operational control as a device to strengthen its claim to the special warfare mission and its justification for organic Army aviation.[33]

JCS again deferred a final decision. On 30 March 1963 the Joint Chiefs informed the Secretary of Defense that they generally accepted the idea that STRICOM could make valuable contributions to the improvement of joint special warfare capabilities. However, the current practice of making units available to STRICOM on a temporary basis should continue until the Army Special Forces expanded or more units became combat ready. At such time, JCS would again review the desirability of passing operational control of a working force of Army and Air Force special warfare units to STRICOM.[34]

The question of an initial working force was resolved on 16 August 1963 when Secretary McNamara approved in principle the assignment to STRICOM of all military responsibilities for the geographical area of the Middle East, Africa south of the Sahara, and Southern Asia (MEAFSA). In September JCS assigned these responsibilities to STRICOM and approved the assignment of U.S.-based, MEAFSA-oriented special warfare forces of the Army and the Air Force to the operational control of CINCSTRIKE. JCS developed the major milestones and schedules for implementing the transfer of functions, and on 28 October the President approved the necessary revision and updating of the Unified Command Plan (UCP).[35]

On 28 November CINCSTRIKE requested information from JCS on the size, composition, designation, and operational readiness date of the special warfare forces to be assigned. In turn, JCS on 30 November asked the services to supply this information. The Air Force had no MEAFSA-oriented special warfare units, but the Special Air Warfare Center possessed a sizeable body of personnel with expertise in the MEAFSA area. After coordinating with TAC, on 20 December the Air Staff decided to organize a special air warfare detachment of the 1st Air Commando Group with an authorization of 16 aircraft (8 strike/reconnaissance, 4 transport, and 4 utility) and approximately 185 personnel. As soon as the detachment was combat ready, expected about 1 February 1964, the Air Force would pass operational control to CINCSTRIKE.[36]

The Air Force determined that this detachment would be organized with personnel and equipment identified but not "set aside." Thus, STRICOM's MEAFSA requirements could be met from resources of SAWC up to the limit of aircraft and personnel authorized for the detachment while still permitting their use in training for oversea deployment and in expanding U.S-based forces to approved levels. The Air Force assured JCS and CINCSTRIKE that after the latter developed precise requirements for special air warfare forces on the basis of experience in the MEAFSA area, the Air Force would initiate reprogramming or other appropriate actions to meet them.[37]

Operation Swift Strike III, a STRICOM operational exercise conducted during July-August 1963 in the southeastern United States, provided another arena for the Army-Air Force special warfare roles and missions struggle. It was the largest joint test of STRICOM's combat capabilities since its activation two years earlier, involving nearly 100,000 men. During the earliest planning phase, beginning January 1963, the Army objected to a joint unconventional warfare operating base (JUWOB) as a coordinating and control element subordinate to a joint unconventional warfare task force (JUWTF). Despite the fact that both elements were successfully utilized during 1962 in Swift Strike II, the Army maintained that the JUWOB was not a part of approved Army doctrine, was a violation of the principles of unified/joint operations, and unduly infringed upon the accomplishment of its unconventional warfare (UW) responsibilities. The Army insisted that a special forces operating base (SFOB)--a unilateral Army element--was the only coordinating and control element required below the JUWTF.

On the other hand, the Air Force's Tactical Air Command informed STRICOM that it was imperative that a joint operational staff be established subordinate to the JUWTF, to insure proper coordination and execution. TAC pointed out that during UW operations the tactical situation constantly changed and so should procedures, tactics, and techniques. Responsibility for these continuing adjustments, TAC maintained, could not be assumed by an SFOB since it was a unilateral Army element, primarily concerned with control of ground warfare. Additionally, TAC advocated a JUWOB because of its apprehension that the Army was attempting to usurp the air role in the UW phase of special warfare.[38]

On 1 March 1963 CINCSTRIKE settled the argument, informing the services that he would organize a JUWTF composed of STRICOM, Army, and Air Force personnel. He directed the Army to operate an SFOB as the command post for the Army UW component and the Air Force to establish an Air Force operating base (AFOB) to perform a similar function for its forces. CINCST withheld a decision as to whether the two operating bases would be collocated or placed at separate locations.[39]

CINCSTRIKE's decision disturbed TAC. In a message to the Air Force Chief of Staff, TAC labeled the creation of separate operating bases a successful Army attempt to eliminate joint command and coordinating structures at the operational level and warned that concepts utilized in exercises often resulted in establishing approved doctrine. TAC stated that the Army's objections to the JUWOB concept and its insistence that all Army resources be located on and utilized from an SFOB stemmed from the

Army goal to expand its air capability. The Air Staff, although agreeing with the TAC position, decided to fight the battle of joint-or-unilateral control during the evaluation period following the exercise. When Swift Strike III was carried out, the SFOB and the AFOB were collocated but separately operated at Laurenburg-Maxton Air Field, S.C.[40]

On 11 May 1963, as TAC had predicted, the Army moved to increase its UW air capability. The Continental Army Command (CONARC) commander informed CINCSTRIKE of his concern over plans for air support of UW operations in Swift Strike III and complained that Army aviation was in danger of being slighted. He told CINCSTRIKE that he intended to provide the participating Army UW group with a detachment of 16 aircraft (4 Caribou's, 2 H-34's, 2 H-13's, and 8 Heliocouriers) and requested that the UW annex be modified to include utilization of Army aviation by the SFOB. He insisted that this detachment would complement, not supersede, Air Force units; USAF aircraft would move the bulk of the personnel and equipment while Army aircraft would be limited to situations and circumstances where their "characteristics and close control provide unique advantages."[41]

CINCSTRIKE replied noncommittally that he had no responsibility for special warfare forces until the Army made them available for participation in training exercises, and he explained that his concern with the equipment they possessed was confined to the impact it would have on joint operations. He made no reference to the request to revise the UW annex of the Swift Strike III plan and gave no indication whether he would use Army aviation for UW operations once the special forces group came under his operational control.[42]

On 15 June 1963, after discussing the matter with both the TAC and

CONARC commanders, CINCSTRIKE rejected the request that the Army air detachment be used in UW operations. Instead, he decided to utilize the unit to support the counterinsurgency effort of the 1st Cavalry Squadron--Joint Task Force Red. He based his decision on a real shortage of aircraft to support counterinsurgency, whereas there was adequate support for the joint UW task force. At the same time, CINCSTRIKE informed the CONARC commander that he was aware of the current roles and missions dispute, and he reminded the Army of the necessity of his maintaining complete objectivity and neutrality if the entire concept of STRICOM was not to be invalidated.[43]

On 25 June the Army Vice Chief of Staff, Gen. Barksdale Hamlett, discussed the subject in a letter to the USAF Vice Chief, Gen. William F. McKee. In outlining the Army's position, he proposed a thesis that would virtually remove the Air Force from UW operations. He quoted the current Joint Strategic Capabilities Plan (JSCP) as assigning the Army "primary responsibility for the development of the doctrine, tactics, techniques, procedures and equipment employed by guerrilla forces in combat operations on land, and the conduct of training of such forces with the assistance of the other Services." He claimed that the JSCP charged the Air Force, Navy, and Marines with providing support and assistance for guerrilla warfare as appropriate and as required. According to General Hamlett, escape and evasion was the only portion of UW operations to which the document assigned the Air Force executive responsibility. Nowhere in this joint document, he continued, was it stated or implied that the Army could not use aircraft in furthering the UW mission: "In fact, it is quite clear from the JSCP that the Army is responsible for providing from its own resources the Army type of equipment and forces required."

General Hamlett refuted the Air Force contention that OSD in August 1962 had barred organic aviation from Army Special Forces by rejecting the aviation brigade. Rather, the Army had interpreted this action to mean that it was to use general purpose aviation for the special warfare mission, and it was precisely on this basis that the Army was incorporating general purpose aviation into its Special Forces groups.* The aircraft proposed for use in Swift Strike III were the same types that would become organic components of the group.

Based on these arguments, General Hamlett suggested to CINCSTRIKE that the Air Force special air warfare unit be used to support the 1st Cavalry Squadron in the counterinsurgency role rather than to support the Army's UW detachment. To meet the UW requirements, he recommended the use of the Army aviation unit, plus support from normal TAC resources. By so doing, the Army Special Forces group, with its newly acquired Army aviation, would be employed as an organizational entity, with operational control exercised by the commander through the SFOB.[44]

General McKee did not continue the discussion. On 12 July the USAF Vice Chief reaffirmed the Air Force position with CINCSTRIKE and informed General Hamlett that the basic Army-Air Force disagreement went much deeper than Swift Strike III and could not be resolved by correspondence. CINCSTRIKE remained firm on his 15 June decision, and the Army attempt to take over air support for the UW portion of Swift Strike III failed.[45]

Preparation of the after-action report on Swift Strike III in August 1963 reopened the issue of joint or unilateral control as it pertained to operating bases. The army insisted that separate operating bases had worked

---

*See above, pp 13-14.

well and recommended that STRICOM continue the concept in future exercises. In fact the Army saw no need even for collocating these bases. The Air Force disagreed, stating that the separate concept had resulted in a lack of operational efficiency and needless cost because of the necessity of duplicating personnel and equipment. A properly organized JUWOB would have eliminated this. The administrative area of the SFOB was too remote from the AFOB for flexibility and timely response, and the physical separation of the two operating bases required duplication of communication nets between Laurenburg-Maxton and JUWTF headquarters. Consequently, the Air Force recommended that the concept of separate AFOB and SFOB facilities be abandoned and that, prior to conducting future exercises, a concept for organizing and operating a JUWOB be developed.[46]

There were 11 divergencies in the preliminary after-action-report. All but three of these divergencies--those associated with the JUWOB concept--were settled quickly to the Air Force's satisfaction at a meeting of Joint Special Warfare Coordinating Group on 21 October 1963. Prior to the meeting the Air Staff decided to change its position on the establishment of a JUWOB for future operational exercises, calling instead for the collocation of the SFOB and AFOB with maximum joint utilization of facilities. The Air Staff made this decision because it knew that the JUWOB concept was completely unacceptable to the Army and that agreement on collocation--a large improvement over separate locations--was the most that it could expect. Further, the Air Force realized that getting the Army to agree to collocation would reinforce the appropriateness of the Air Force role in UW and weaken the Army justification for organic aircraft.[47]

At the 21 October meeting the Air Force emphasized the need for close coordination at the SFOB-AFOB level of joint UW operations, pointed out the rightful Air Force role in UW, and highlighted the impact and consequences of Army efforts to acquire organic aviation for UW operations. The Air Force called for a joint organization to provide the base support for a collocated SFOB-AFOB, creation of a common communication facility to include a single side-band link to aircraft, and placement of USAF personnel on full-time liaison in the operations element of the SFOB to insure timely USAF knowledge of requirements.

Complete agreement could not be reached, but the Air Force position was accepted in principle, and the Swift Strike III SFOB and AFOB commanders were instructed to meet the following day and draw up jointly acceptable procedures for improving SFOB-AFOB coordination in future exercises. The JSWCG meeting reflected in miniature the divergent views of the Army and Air Force across the range of special warfare and tactical air concepts. Although the JUWTF after-action-report was revised to be acceptable to both services, the major issues of roles and missions still remained.[48]

II. EXPANDING SPECIAL AIR WARFARE CAPABILITIES

The Air Force was aware that special warfare requirements of early 1963 exceeded resources. SAWC manning could not support the growing demands in Southeast Asia and the Caribbean area, much less tentative requirements in the Middle East and elsewhere. Throughout the year, requirements continued to grow and the Air Force endeavored to expand its SAW forces to meet the needs.

On 1 January 1963 the Special Air Warfare Center had an authorized strength of 2,167 primary element personnel: Headquarters--31, 1st Combat Applications Group--51, and 1st Air Commando Group (including the Farmgate and Bold Venture detachments)--2,085. The 1st Air Commando Group had 138 aircraft authorized and the composite squadron an additional 46, for a total of 184.[*1]

Assigned strengths were far lower. Headquarters SAWC possessed 33 men; the 1st Combat Applications Group--temporarily manned with personnel borrowed from the Air Proving Ground Center and the Army--had none officially assigned; and the 1st Air Commando Group contained 965 men. The assigned SAWC aircraft totaled 103--66 in the United States, 24 in South Vietnam, and 13 in Panama. In addition, two TAC C-123 assault transport squadrons deployed to South Vietnam totaled 235 personnel and 32 aircraft. The Ranch Hand detachment of spray-equipped C-123's, deployed in December 1961 to conduct defoliation experiments on the SVN jungles, had 19 personnel

---

*See above, pp 4 and 7n.

and 3 aircraft. Early in the SVN special warfare action, PACAF dispatched a detachment (Able Mable) of 4 RF-101's to Thailand where it performed photoreconnaissance for all Southeast Asia. By the beginning of 1963 the detachment had moved to South Vietnam.[2]

Buildup of Units

SAWC Reorganization

Within the United States the Air Force reorganized SAWC to conform to the 6-squadron/184-aircraft structure authorized for special air warfare forces by PCP-2 in November 1962. On 30 April 1963, TAC activated and organized the 602d Fighter Squadron (Commando) under the 1st Air Commando Group. On 1 July it activated the 603d and 604th Fighter Squadrons (Commando) as part of the 1st ACG, and on 15 November the 605th Air Commando Squadron, Composite. TAC attached the 605th to USAF Southern Command (USAFSO) for operational control and assigned the unit to Howard AFB, Panama.[3]

On 1 June 1963 TAC redesignated the 1st Air Commando Group the 1st Air Commando Wing. At the same time, TAC redesignated the 1st Combat Applications Group as a wing, but the redesignation was withdrawn when Headquarters USAF decided that the action was not appropriate to the unit's mission or its strength.[4]

PACAF*

In September 1962 the demand for special warfare air support in South Vietnam exceeded Air Force capabilities, and PACAF proposed to CINCPAC that

---

*A more complete coverage of special air warfare in South Vietnam appears in the forthcoming AFCHO study, *Air Operations in South Vietnam, 1961-1963*, by Jacob Van Staaveren.

Farmgate be augmented with 5 T-28's, 10 B-26's, 2 C-47's, and 117 personnel. CINCPAC agreed and on 2 November recommended to JCS the proposed increase--plus one additional B-26. JCS supported this recommendation but deleted the B-26, and Secretary McNamara approved it on 28 December. President Kennedy approved the action, and in February 1963 the Air Force reported the augmentation completed. At this point, Farmgate contained 41 aircraft and 275 personnel, with a ratio of 1.5 crews per aircraft.[5]

On 7 January, while the augmentation was under way, the commander of Military Assistance Command, Vietnam (MACV) asked for additional aircraft to support a three-year plan designed to defeat the Viet Cong by 1966 and to make South Vietnam responsible for their own defense by that date. He requested a third TAC transport squadron of 16 C-123's; a squadron of 25 T-28's; a squadron of 25 B-26's; and three tactical air support squadrons, each with 22 U-10's, to increase air surveillance and improve forward air control capabilities. CINCPAC was in accord on the transport squadron but suggested that a better solution for strike aircraft (T-28/B-26) would be to increase the number of pilots and maintenance crews in Farmgate. He also recommended only two rather than three U-10 squadrons (or equivalent).[6]

JCS agreed to the deployment of the third C-123 squadron and the plan to increase Farmgate personnel. However, faced with strenuous claims from both the Army and the Air Force over who should deploy and operate the tactical air support squadrons, JCS finally accepted a CINCPAC compromise recommendation that the Air Force should deploy one of the squadrons and the Army the other. Because of the limited number of U-10's in the inventory, TO-1D's (L-19's) were substituted.* Secretary McNamara approved on

---
*In addition, JCS approved a buildup of Army aviation: a platoon of U'1's, 15 additional O-1A's for Army helicopter companies and support of corps advisers, and 10 UH-13 helicopters.

26 March and on 1 April the Air Staff instructed TAC to begin implementation.[7]

The lengthy period of deliberation preceding the expansion decision stemmed from a controversy over the service that should provide aircraft for the roles of tactical air reconnaissance, forward air control, and support liaison. Throughout the episode, the Air Force found itself in the unusual and unique position of wanting to continue its responsibility for these functions although it did not have the proper aircraft to do so. On the other hand, the Army was "loud and clear in its position that, not only were the MACV/CINCPAC mission requirements for low slow aircraft their backyard, but they had the in-house capability to organize and deploy two complete companies without delay." Even when the Air Force finally won responsibility for deploying one of the two tactical air support squadrons, it had to borrow TO-1D's from the Army to equip that unit.[8]

TO-1D pilot training began at Hurlburt Field in June 1963, and the first group of 22 completed the course by the end of the month. On 17 June the Air Force constituted and activated the 19th Tactical Air Support Squadron (L), and on 9 July the unit was organized at Bien Hoa AB, South Vietnam. The first four TO-1D's were airlifted into the theater early in July, the remaining aircraft arriving by ship in August.[9]

With the augmentation approved in March, the authorized USAF force in Vietnam included three C-123 squadrons, Farmgate with its 41 assorted aircraft, and the 19th Tactical Air Support Squadron equipped with 22 TO-1D's. This large force required a permanent command relationship rather than "temporary duty" arrangements, in order to stabilize manning, reduce training requirements, and exploit more fully the operational experience of personnel now being lost after six months of TDY. Accordingly, on 8 April the Air Force requested JCS to approve the permanent assignment to PACAF of all TAC units on TDY in South Vietnam. This involved 198 personnel in the tactical air support unit, 474 in Farmgate, and approximately 1,034 in the troop carrier squadrons--including aerial spray and command support. JCS approved on 12 April.[10]

The Air Force then activated Farmgate as a permanent unit under PACAF. Activating the 1st Air Commando Squadron, Composite on 17 June, the Air Force organized it at Bien Hoa AB on 9 July. The new unit, with an authorized strength of 474 personnel and 41 aircraft, became a part of the 34th Tactical Group, 2d Air Division. The Air Force directed TAC to replace current temporary personnel with permanent personnel as quickly as possible and to operate SAWC training facilities at maximum capability to complete this task. The first PCS aircrew contingent for the commando squadron entered training in June 1963 and departed for South Vietnam in August. The prescribed crew ratio of 2 per aircraft was attained in October, and full permanent party status was set for early 1964.[11]

The two TAC C-123 squadrons, plus the three C-123 Ranch Hand aircraft had formed the Air Transport Squadron, Provisional 2 in May 1962, and the 464th Troop Carrier Wing at Pope AFB, N.C., supplied personnel on a 179-day rotational basis. This continuing requirement was beyond TAC's capability without rotating personnel for repeat tours. After the March decision to place a third C-123 squadron (SAW Buck VII) in South Vietnam was carried out, the Air Force programmed all three squadrons for conversion from temporary to permanent-change-of-station status on 1 July 1963. To provide an acceptable commitment of sorties and flying hours per tour, the Air Force increased crew ratio from 1.25 to 1.5 and instituted a 12-month tour.[12]

During 1963 PACAF increased and consolidated air reconnaissance forces in South Vietnam. In March, four RB-26's (Sweet Sue) deployed to augment the Farmgate detachment. On 6 May, two RB-57's (Patricia Lynn) arrived in the theater. On 4 November PACAF merged all SAW reconnaissance aircraft (including Able Mable) into one detachment at Tan Son Nhut AB.[13]

The Air Force's primary training goal in Vietnam was to develop a self-sufficient VNAF that would allow the withdrawal of U.S. units. A major obstacle was the lack of trained VNAF pilots and maintenance personnel. In March 1963 the VNAF had 243 pilots and a requirement of 441 to operate 185 assigned aircraft. By the end of fiscal year 1964, the requirement would total 570 pilots to man 220 aircraft.[14]

Prior to 1963 all VNAF pilot training took place in the United States. To speed the job, Air Force leaders late in 1962 began pressing for in-country training. The SVN government supported the Air Force, since in-country training would eliminate displacement of trainees, would afford the pilots better knowledge of the terrain over which they would operate, and would save trainee transit time to and from the United States.[15]

Early in March PACAF submitted to CINCPAC the Air Force's proposal for the establishment of in-country primary pilot training. CINCPAC forwarded the proposal on 15 March and asked JCS to establish a USAF light aircraft training unit--consisting of 29 officers, 84 enlisted men, and 25 U-17A's (Cessna 185)--to operate under the control of the Military Assistance Advisory Group--Vietnam (MAAG-V). The unit would provide primary training for 50 pilots each 90 days, and follow-on training would be

33

done in T-28, AD-6, and C-47 aircraft. The plan was not an attempt to change the general character of training, and the Air Force had no intention of instituting it on a permanent basis. There would be no change in the type and amount of training, only a relocation of facilities to South Vietnam. The Air Force envisioned in-country training as a temporary expedient, for a period of about 18 to 24 months. Once sufficient numbers of VNAF pilots were trained, assistance would cease. MAAG advisers and possibly short-term mobile training teams could undertake conversion training as new aircraft were introduced. On 25 April, JCS approved the CINCPAC request.[16]

On 27 May Secretary McNamara directed the Air Force to expedite the in-country training program. The Air Force then arranged to purchase 25 U-17A's, and Air Training Command (ATC) began working with the Cessna Aircraft Company to prepare instructor liaison pilots and maintenance personnel. On 28 June the Air Force authorized ATC to begin training USAF Field Training Detachment (FTD) 921R, consisting of 29 officers and 84 airmen. Twenty officers were instructor pilots, and the balance served as academic, operations, and maintenance instructors. Nearly all of the 84 airmen were maintenance specialists. The Air Force planned to have all VNAF students receive 80 hours of flying training and 185 hours of academic instruction. The course would prepare students for a specific job to be accomplished in a specific area, and it would qualify them as contact daytime liaison pilots. Preflight training in South Vietnam got under way on 1 September and the first class of 50 pilots began flight training on 1 October.[17]

In January 1963 the Air Force had deployed to South Vietnam helicopter FTD 917H with 59 men. In February the unit began crosstraining 15

VNAF fixed-wing pilots as helicopter instructors, using eight VNAF H-19's. In line with expanded in-country training, CINCPAC on 8 May requested the Air Force to enlarge this detachment. The Air Force agreed and on 28 June authorized ATC to augment FTD 917H with 11 officers and 31 airmen and directed MATS to deliver nine additional H-19's--currently assigned to units in Europe. This augmentation allowed the number of pilot trainees in each five-month class to double--from 15 to 30.[18]

By the end of 1963 the Air Force had nearly 500 SVN students engaged in English language training, preparatory to undergoing pilot or technical courses. Fifty student pilots training in U-17A's were near the end of a 16-week course, 67 pilots were or had completed transition training in C-47 aircraft, and 7 student pilots were attending schools in the United States.*[19]

USAFE

Until mid-1963 CINCEUR had not indicated any definite requirements for special air warfare forces in his theater. In fact, as late as February 1963, Gen. Truman H. Landon, CINCUSAFE, stated that the need for such forces was not "readily apparent." The Air Staff felt, however, that there was a need and included a composite squadron of 30 aircraft in PCP-3, the unit to be available to USAFE in fiscal year 1965. Before the Secretary of Defense reached a decision on the PCP, demands to support numerous mobile training teams and provide air support to the Army's 10th Special

---

*By June 1964 FTD 921R had trained 93 pilots and had 26 pilots and 32 maintenance personnel in training. FTD 917H had trained 69 pilots and 62 mechanics and had 30 pilots and 31 mechanics in training. (Hq USAF Daily Staff Digest, 19 Jun 64.)

Forces Group caused both CINCEUR and CINCUSAFE to change their views.* On 11 June 1963, CINCEUR asked JCS to establish an interim composite SAW unit in EUCOM at an early date in fiscal year 1964. CINCEUR suggested a detachment of 150 to 180 personnel (excluding base and logistical support personnel) and 16 aircraft (6 C-47's, 4 C-123's, and 6 U-10A's).[20]

The Air Force on 20 July agreed that CINCEUR's request was valid but pointed out to JCS that currently stated requirements of the unified commanders were already taxing the approved 6-squadron/184-aircraft force. The Air Force Chief of Staff therefore pressed for approval of PCP-3, then under consideration by JCS, to cover fiscal year 1965 requirements and urged reprogramming of the SAW forces to meet CINCEUR's needs in the interim.[21]

On 24 July JCS approved the dispatch of an interim SAW detachment to Europe in late fiscal year 1964, and the Air Force began preparations for its training and deployment. Five days later, JCS sent PCP-3 to SOD for action. On 16 August, however, Secretary McNamara decided to assign all military responsibilities in the MEAFSA area to STRICOM.† This relieved CINCEUR of responsibility for much of the area in the Middle East where requirements for SAW operations were the highest--particularly counterinsurgency actions and training.

On 3 December 1963 the new CINCUSAFE, Gen. Gabriel P. Disosway, observed that the change in responsibilities, coupled with DOD efforts to decrease the "gold flow," raised questions on the advisability of deploying

---

*See above, p 8.

†See above, p 20.

a special air warfare unit into the European theater. He suggested that the minimal CINCEUR requirements could best be handled by a combination of in-theater airlift, temporary transfer of SAW forces on a case-by-case basis, establishment of a U.S.-based composite air strike force (CASF) of SAW units, and augmentation by the Air National Guard/USAF Reserve in the event of general war. Disosway recommended that the Air Staff reevaluate the decision to send a unit to Europe.[22]

The Air Staff disagreed with CINCUSAFE's proposal, and on 28 December General McKee, Vice Chief of Staff, informed General Disosway that a unit would be deployed. There were a number of reasons why the Air Force had proceeded with plans to deploy the SAW unit to Europe despite the shift of responsibility from CINCEUR to CINCSTRIKE and the unfavorable effect on the gold-flow problem. The original objective of assigning USAFE a SAW unit was to provide a capability for both counterinsurgency and unconventional warfare operations. While the realignment had limited drastically or possibly voided the counterinsurgency requirement in EUCOM, the requirement for an unconventional warfare capability continued to exist. In fact, CINCEUR on several occasions had expressed concern both with the inadequacy of air support for unconventional warfare training and with the lack of sufficient D-day airlift to support the unconventional warfare and clandestine intelligence collection activities called for in CINCEUR operational plans. This dissatisfaction had reached a climax in June 1963 with CINCEUR's request for a composite SAW unit. The Air Force had supported this requirement when it was considered favorably by JCS in July, and it constituted one reason for urging OSD to approve PCP-3.[23]

General McKee feared that the Army would use the lack of adequate SAW capability in USAFE as a reason for adding its own aviation equipment as an organic part of the 10th Special Forces Group. He also pointed out that CINCEUR had not proposed redeployment of the 10th in the gold-flow actions. Should this unit be returned to the United States, the Air Staff would reexamine the requirement for a Europe-based special air warfare unit. In closing, General McKee noted that on 26 December Deputy Secretary of Defense Gilpatric had approved the interim SAW detachment for Europe, to consist of 2 C-47's, 6 U-10's, and 4 C-123's--or any combination of these aircraft not to exceed 12--and a maximum of 150 people.[24]

CAIRC/USAFSO*

Special air warfare forces in Latin America during most of 1963 consisted of the small Bold Venture detachment deployed in May 1962. On 1 January 1963 it contained 13 aircraft and 75 men and served as the nucleus for the SAW activities in the area. PCP-2, approved on 24 November 1962, had authorized a composite squadron of 46 aircraft (8 T-28's, 8 B-26's, 12 C-46's, 12 C-47's, and 6 U-10B's) and 548 personnel, but buildup of the force was slow and by June 1963 there were still only 92 personnel and 14 aircraft in the area. On 24 October the Air Force directed TAC to activate the 605th Air Commando Squadron, Composite for operations in Latin America. Accomplishing this on 15 November at Howard AFB, Panama, TAC attached the squadron to USAFSO for operational control, directed the 605th to absorb the Bold Venture detachment, and insured that trained personnel would arrive in step with the availability of aircraft and facilities at Howard between January and November 1964. Housing at the base had to be vacated by the Army prior to the movement of Air Force personnel.[25]

---

*On 1 May 1963 the U.S. Caribbean Command became the U.S. Southern Command. Consequently, on 8 July, the Air Force redesignated the Caribbean Air Command (CAIRC) the United States Air Forces Southern Command (USAFSO).

Civic Actions

Early in its special air warfare planning, the Air Force recognized that prevention or defeat of subversion and insurgency called for more than military operations alone but rather included civic actions as well.* The principle involved in civic action was clear and familiar. As General LeMay, in October 1963, stated:[26]

> An Air Force which identifies itself with the progress and well being of the populace will be accorded public goodwill, respect and support . . . . By encouraging and helping the Air Forces of friendly governments make their civic action contribution, we can demonstrate increasingly the superiority of free government on the basis of hard achievements, as well as moral values. In this way our prospects are improved for preventing or relieving the conditions of unrest which could be exploited by insurgent elements in conducting guerrilla operations.

American military units overseas joined in many types of community projects that directly supported the military objective of forestalling revolutions and Communist uprisings, with each military service contributing its peculiar skills and talents.[27]

At Dhahran Air Base, in Saudi Arabia, the Air Force converted a hangar into a classroom for the children of Saudi Arabian airmen. USAF officers and their wives taught the children first aid, handicrafts, American history, and English. In Ethiopia and Greece, USAF personnel tested local water supplies. In Greece and Morocco, the Air Force assisted local workers in constructing wells and distributing water. Specially equipped

---

*JCS official definition: Military civic action--The use of preponderantly indigenous military forces on projects useful to the local population at all levels in such fields as education, training, public works, agriculture, transportation, communications, health, sanitation, and others contributing to economic and social development, which would also serve to improve the standing of the military forces with the population. (US forces may at times advise or engage in military civic actions in overseas areas.) (JCS Pub 1, Ch 1, 2 Jul 62.)

C-123's sprayed insecticides over crops in the perpetual war on locusts in Iran and Thailand. In Turkey, over 155,000 conscripts were taught to read and write by the U.S. Air Force during the past three years. In South Vietnam, USAF personnel advised or engaged in numerous civic actions. Projects at the hamlet and village level were most successful, including such activities as constructing and equipping schools, providing medical treatment, drilling wells, and increasing agricultural production.[28]

The Air Force's greatest civic action effort was in Latin America. As of 30 June 1963, USAFSO was supervising 14 USAF missions, one section of a joint military commission, and one section of a military assistance advisory group. Most of these units, in being since World War II or shortly after, had for a number of years successfully excluded non-Western Hemisphere military influences from Latin America. However, with the revolution in Cuba and the replacement there of the USAF mission, numbering approximately 15 persons, by a Soviet mission, containing several thousands, the task throughout all of Latin America had become much more difficult. To counteract this Communist threat, the Air Force initiated an active civic action program within the air forces of the Latin American nations--sparked by the missions and the SAW forces. Airmen, aircraft, and air facilities were uniquely qualified to provide technical training, transportation, communications, preventive medicine, weather information, crop-dusting, insect and rodent control, and other economic and social services for a military civic action program. They could reduce the demand for expensive (and prestige) weapon systems, promote internal security by eliminating causes of dissidence and unrest, and identify military forces with, not against, the needs and aspirations of the people.[29]

In those countries where Air Force personnel had been stationed, routine preventive medicine and sanitation surveys showed the urgent need for basic medical services to the populations. USAFSO recommended that Latin American air forces provide properly trained and equipped preventive medicine teams to reduce the high sickness and fatality rates prevalent in remote areas of their countries. Since these air forces would then be identified as having a humanitarian interest in local populations, the U.S. Air Force encouraged the use of airpower in fighting disease.

With this objective in mind, the air forces of the Latin American nations gave major emphasis during 1963 to preventive medicine in their civic action programs. For instance, since the isolation of the people in the Chilean provinces of Osorno and Aysen aggravated their health and welfare problems, the Chilean Air Force dispatched a medical team to the region every two months. The medical care included all phases of dental and preventive medicine, including immunizations, and the air force air-evacuated serious cases. The program was operated in conjunction with the Chilean Department of Health and Welfare. The Guatemalan Air Force provided major support to medical and public health projects throughout the little country. One project involved the opening and operation of a medical clinic at La Aurora Airport for the Indian laborers in the area. In addition, the air force painted and labeled as public health vehicles one C-45 and two Cessna 180's. The aircraft carried medical teams to epidemic or disaster areas and served as ambulances when required.[30]

To enhance the scope of this type of activity, USAFSO on 2 October 1962, proposed a preventive medicine training program at the USAF School for Latin America, Albrook AFB, Panama. Latin American air force officials enthusiasticlly indorsed the plan during a March 1963 conference, and USAFSO submitted it to CINCSOUTHCOM, who approved and forwarded it to JCS and OSD. OSD authorized initial funding of $250,000 in MAP funds, and on 8 July the program began with 46 students from eight Latin American countries.* Medical teams from the air forces of Bolivia, Paraguay, Venezuela, Nicaragua, the Dominican Republic, Honduras, Guatemala, and Ecuador participated. Basically, the program was designed to train five-man teams, including two veterinary technicians, two medical service technicians, and one laboratory technician. With the addition of a doctor, each team had the capability to function as a small dispensary. Following the six-month course--completed in December 1963--the respective air forces, utilizing MAP-supplied Cessna 185's, transported these teams to remote areas of their countries to provide on-the-spot medical treatment, sanitation instruction, and air evacuation services. They formed a welcome and beneficial contact between the military and civilian populations and proved a valid counter against Communist-inspired unrest.[31]

Later phases of the preventive medicine program included plans to outfit a C-47 flying dispensary and to obtain additional helicopters that could reach areas without airstrips. The 1st Combat Applications Group field-tested in Panama and Guatemala a medical dispensary transportable in a U-10. It proved successful and added to the deployment kit of the Special Air Warfare Center.†[32]

---

*Eventual cost of the program, including the cost of the aircraft, was estimated at $6.3 million.

†On 6 January 1964, 34 Latin American air force students--representing Ecuador, Panama, Paraguay, Nicaragua, El Salvador, Bolivia, Venezuela, and Guatemala--entered the second class of preventive medicine. Thirteen of these students were assigned courses in instructional techniques to enable them to train personnel of their own air forces. (Sup 132 to AF Policy Ltr for Comdrs, Jun 64.)

USAF efforts to promote civic actions under indigenous air force sponsorship were also successful in providing air transportation, communication, and mail services to remote and isolated regions. In Columbia, for example, the air force organized and operated a government-owned airline, consisting of one C-47, two PBY's, and two L-20's. Established on 12 April 1962, the airline's intended purpose was to foster economic and social development in underdeveloped regions by providing improved transportation service and moving personnel, mail, and equipment at very low rates. The Agency for International Development (AID) scheduled delivery of six C-47's and four C-54's to supplement this inventory, and the USAF mission to Columbia strongly recommended the project.[33]

The Peruvian Air Force operated a commercial-type airline of 12 C-47's and 7 C-46's between coastal and remote mountainous locations. The majority of the routes were not serviced by any other airline or means of transportation. It provided airlift of food, construction equipment, and passengers. Early in 1963, using light amphibious aircraft, it inaugurated airmail service from Iquition to the small, isolated villages along the Amazon River and its tributaries. On 3 August it initiated helicopter service from Lima to remote villages not served by other means of transportation. On biweekly trips, the helicopters delivered mail, medicines, and other items of necessity to these communities. These services contributed to the economic growth of Peru and, at the same time, enhanced the prestige of the Peruvian Air Force in the eyes of its countrymen.[34]

With the encouragement of USAF advisers, the transport squadron of the Nicaraguan Air Force took civic action as its primary mission. The squadron carried tons of building materials and foodstuffs to remote locations and provided transportation for doctors, dentists, and sanitation experts. The El Salvadoran Air Force, although small and operating under a limited budget, accepted the idea of civic action and developed several worthwhile projects to assist the economy of the country and increase its own stature in the eyes of the people. For example, it carried out crop-dusting as needed and transported several tons of hybrid corn from Mexico.[35]

Utilizing its point-to-point radio facilities, the Chilian Air Force established long-line telephone communications for the isolated Aysen-Chiloe provinces, bringing these regions into direct contact with the rest of the country. The United States through its military assistance program (MAP) supplied and supported some of the equipment.[36]

Mobile Training Teams

To counter Communist insurgency successfully required the willing and able support of the nations under attack. For the United States to attempt to suppress such threats with only its own special warfare forces would have been fruitless. Therefore the United States concentrated on employing its special warfare forces to train the armed forces of the threatened nations. For South Vietnam this meant deploying many officers and men as advisers and instructors. For other areas of the world--where actual fighting had not broken out--the United States provided small mobile training teams (MTT's), many jointly manned by the Air Force and Army.

SAWC's Bold Venture detachment supplied the resources for most of the U.S. Air Force's MTT effort in Latin America. By mid-1963 the Air Force had sent briefing, survey, or MTT training teams to a dozen Latin American nations--Argentina, Bolivia, Brazil, Chile, Colombia, Dominican

Republic, Ecuador, El Salvador, Guatemala, Honduras, Peru, and Venezuela--and obtained excellent results. Although special warfare was a function of the Chilean army and the national police, with the air force providing transportation when needed, the air force requested of the United States and received a joint briefing on special air warfare training. In Colombia, where more than 25,000 lives have been lost in the last decade to internal disorders, the air force increased its support of the army by utilizing H-43B helicopters to suppress bandit groups. Because of the success of this campaign, Colombia's President requested the United States to lend him three additional H-43B's. The three aircraft arrived on 18 May 1963, along with an MTT that assembled, test-flew, and committed them to special warfare operations within 10 days.

A joint special warfare survey team visited Ecuador in March 1963 to determine the needs of the Ecuadorian army and air force. The United States subsequently programmed an air counterinsurgency and an air psychological team to arrive in the country during the spring of 1964. In February 1963 a 16-man MTT completed the training of 25 Guatemalan Air Force personnel. Another MTT arrived in Peru in April 1963 and by June had trained 14 Peruvian B-26 pilots and two technicians in special air warfare techniques. The Air Force had follow-on MTT's scheduled for fiscal years 1964-69.[37]

The demand for MTT's in Latin America far exceeded USAFSO resources. In June the command informed the Air Staff that support of Army Special Forces training in the Canal Zone permitted the deployment of only one MTT elsewhere, whereas minimum obligations during the last six months of 1963 would require simultaneous deployment of at least two MTT's. USAFSO warned that failure to support the Army Special Forces training exercises or meet MTT requirements would almost certainly draw an immediate request for an Army aviation company to fill the void. Meeting fiscal year 1964 MTT requirements therefore hinged on the buildup during January-March 1964 of the 605th Air Commando Squadron* and the timely funding of requested MAP training and material support.[38]

The African and Middle Eastern areas also made demands on USAF's capability to supply special air warfare MTT's. The first MTT--two C-47's and their crews--had gone to Mali, Africa, in late 1961 and successfully trained Malinese soldiers in airborne operations. The second MTT effort for that country began on 21 January 1963, when two C-123's departed Pope AFB, N.C. They were followed two days later by a C-124 carrying supplies and personnel, and all three aircraft were in place by the end of the month. Twenty-seven 1st Air Commando Group personnel participated in this Air Force-Army operation (Sandy Beach II). In the three and a half months that the team spent in Mali, it trained 345 paratroopers and supervised more than 2,000 jumps. The MTT completed its task in May and returned to the United States.[39]

On 1 February, 12 personnel from the 1st Air Commando Group departed (without aircraft) for Saudi Arabia to participate in a MAP-approved joint-service MTT. Their primary mission was to train Arab crews flying C-47's and C-123's in assault landings and takeoffs, low-level navigation, resupply procedures, and infiltration and exfiltration of personnel. The MTT completed the work successfully on 24 March and returned to the United States.[40]

In March the Air Force participated with the Army in two additional

---

*See above, p 29, 38.

MTT operations. On the 7th, seven personnel from the 1st Air Commando Group departed for Greece to train the Royal Hellenic Air Force in conducting psychological, unconventional, and counterinsurgency warfare. On the 18th a team of two USAF specialists went to Iran to instruct Iranian army personnel on the role of airpower in special warfare.[41]

Fiscal year 1964 MTT requirements for the African-Middle Eastern area were high. CINCEUR, who was responsible for the region until late in 1963, used these requirements as partial justification for his June 1963 request that JCS assign a special air warfare unit to USAFE.* Nine MTT's were already programmed to the area: four to Iran (for periods of 9, 8, 4, and 10 weeks respectively), one to Jordan (12 weeks), one to Ethiopia (8 weeks), one to Turkey (8 weeks), one to Saudi Arabia (8 weeks), and one to Pakistan (8 weeks).[42]

About the same time, both the SAWC and TAC commanders expressed concern that current MTT requirements might overdraw from the overall special air warfare program. In June TAC informed the Air Staff of this concern and suggested that MTT's be planned and developed on a long-term basis. TAC pointed out that on several occasions when SAWC had formed MTT's to meet specific but unprogrammed requirements a corresponding reduction in other SAWC capabilities had resulted. Moreover, TAC believed that this "piecemeal impromptu approach" would never really satisfy requirements.[43]

TAC reported that current MTT assistance was totally inadequate in most areas of the world--both in terms of availability and scope of training operations--and reminded the Air Staff that neither SAWC's mission nor plans called for MTT's. As a corrective measure, TAC proposed on 26 July

---

*See above, pp 35-36.

that it establish at SAWC a special MTT unit of 131 men, divided into 10 area-oriented MTT's. The Air Staff disapproved the proposal. It admitted that MTT operations had been impromptu in the past but pointed out that PCP-3, then under consideration in OSD, called for composite units in EUCOM, PACOM, and SOUTHCOM to provide theater capabilities. The necessity for this in-house MTT capability was used by the unified commanders in establishing their requirements for SAW units--and by the Air Force to justify PCP-3.[44]

The President's trip to West Germany in June 1963 stimulated increased emphasis on the use of MTT's. President Kennedy was "tremendously impressed" with the Special Forces group he found there. On 15 July he praised them to Secretary McNamara but raised a question on the wisdom of a 1,000-man unit being stationed in Germany, virtually on garrison duty. He asked if it would not be a good idea to send them on training missions throughout Latin America, Africa, Asia, or the Middle East to demonstrate and train personnel of the underdeveloped nations in counteracting Communist insurgency.[45]

Immediately, JCS advised CINCEUR, CINCPAC, and CINCSOUTHCOM of the President's interest and asked for a report on the extent special warfare forces in their theaters were being used for this purpose. On 16 July the Air Force Chief of Staff notified the air component commanders and requested that they emphasize USAF contributions to and the need for joint operations in their reports to the unified commander. Based on the comments from the theater commanders and service chiefs, the JCS Chairman on 24 July prepared a report for the President. The Air Force was not pleased with its contents, since a lengthy account of USAF activities submitted by the Chief of Staff was almost entirely omitted.[46]

At a meeting with the JCS on 24 July the President reaffirmed his views of the Army Special Forces and expressed his satisfaction with MTT activities. The President noted, however, that many MTT's were very small and expressed a desire for larger teams. The Air Force coordinated on a draft JCS message to the unified commanders reflecting the President's views and emphasizing the necessity for jointly manned MTT's. The Chairman of JCS revised this message prior to transmittal, however, limiting its application to Army Special Forces only. Therefore the Air Staff, on 2 August, again advised air component commanders to insure appropriate USAF participation in MTT operations.[47]

The President, realizing that MTT's had diplomatic as well as military overtones, informed the Secretary of State on 26 July that DOD intended to send teams to a number of countries during fiscal year 1964. He stated the belief that their presence would project a U.S. image that would have useful political influence. Since the judgment of U.S. ambassadors in the countries concerned would be dominant in both the decision to introduce the teams and the decision on team size, the President suggested that affected ambassadors be informed well in advance. In response, DOD, AID, and State Department dispatched a joint message on 6 August to each, explaining the potential of MTT's in building internal security and urging their use.[48]

President Kennedy later stated that the message had not been sufficiently directive and asked for a new and stronger one; however, this was not accomplished before his death. On 2 December, two follow-on joint messages were sent, explaining in detail what an MTT could accomplish, emphasizing the President's interest in the program, and delineating the qualifications and availability of U.S. special warfare forces. The Joint Staff drafted these messages and dispatched them without service coordination. Air Force capabilities again received "less than full coverage." In an attempt to overcome this oversight, the Air Staff advised each air attaché about the messages and requested him to insure that USAF capabilities were considered when the ambassador developed internal defense and MAP plans.[49]

Search for Improved Special Air Warfare Aircraft

Beginning in 1961 the Air Force used either World War II types of tactical aircraft or postwar trainer aircraft for special air warfare operations. These aircraft came the closest to meeting combat performance requirements, were available, and were in the inventories of the MAP recipient countries. The Air Force realized, however, that new aircraft would be required as current aircraft became increasingly obsolescent or even obsolete.

In January 1963 TAC had 25 B-26's from World War II in its special air warfare forces. This was less than the number needed to conduct operations in South Vietnam and to train replacement crews. Additionally, the B-26 required modification to improve its capability for the current mission. Early in February 1963, the On-Mark Engineering Corporation delivered a YB-26K to SAWC. This modified aircraft had 14 fixed 50-caliber machine guns--three in each wing and eight in the nose. Eight external pylons provided hang-on space for either 4,000 pounds of bombs or additional fuel tanks. Replacement of the R-2800-27/79 engine with the R-2800-103W provided greater speed and power and, coupled with new wheels and brakes, improved the aircraft's short-runway performance.

After the Air Force had thoroughly tested the YB-26K and found it satisfactory, the Air Staff agreed to modify 40 B-26's to the new configuration, using internally reprogrammed funds. On 22 October the Air Force contracted with On-Mark to deliver one aircraft in March 1964, two or three in April, and four each month thereafter until completion in January 1965.*[50]

In 1962 the Air Force had also proposed to improve its strike/reconnaissance capability with suitable modifications to the T-28, an immediate post-World War II trainer. The Air Force planned a T-28 "growth model" that would possess greater firepower through the addition of six external pylons to carry 3,000 pounds of bombs; have greater performance capability through the installation of the R-1820-26 with a 1,425-horsepower rating; and contain an intelligence capability through the inclusion of a photo-reconnaissance package. However, early in 1963 the Air Force found the R-1820-86 in critically short supply, while the long lead time and high cost of the most suitable substitute--the R-1820-82--was not compatible with the requirement schedules. This, plus the fact that the Navy agreed to release a number of A-1E (AD-5) aircraft for Air Force use, caused the Air Staff to cancel the proposed T-28 "growth" configuration.[51]

The Air Force continued to be interested in a turboprop version of the T-28. North American Aviation Company completed and flew the first YAT-28E test-bed aircraft on 15 February 1963. This prototype was equipped

---

*Slippage during the spring of 1964 caused a 60- to 90-day delay in delivery schedule so that the last aircraft would not be delivered until April 1965.

with a T-55 turboprop engine rated at 2,450 horsepower, which provided increased speed, range, and load-carrying capabilities. The aircraft carried 4,000 pounds of armament, two 50-caliber under-wing machine guns, and other miscellaneous weapons. On 27 March the YAT-28E crashed but not before it had completed about 20 percent of the contractor tests and proved its excellent flying qualities. On 25 April the Chief of Staff approved modifying two additional T-28's to the turboprop configuration, and on 15 November the second YAT-28E made its first flight. After a number of successful test flights, the Air Force in December signed a letter contract for the third YAT-28E, with a projected delivery date of May 1964. When completed, this aircraft would contain self-sealing tanks, armor plate, ejection seats, and all the communication-navigation gear installed in SAWC's regular T-28's.[52]

Late in 1962, in a companion effort to the YAT-28E, the Air Force advocated modifying the T-37 jet as a trainer/MAP/SAW aircraft. It also proposed the YAT-37D as a substitute for a Director of Defense Research and Engineering (DDR&E) proposal to construct a light attack aircraft based on a Marine Corps requirement. In December Deputy Secretary of Defense Gilpatric approved the YAT-37D, as well as the development program favored by DDR&E, instructing the Air Force to submit its modification plan for review.*

The Air Force plan, submitted on 1 February 1963, called for uprating the T-37 by substituting a 2,400-pound-thrust engine and adding six external pylons to carry up to 3,000 pounds of conventional ordnance. In addition the aircraft would have 90-gallon wingtip fuel tanks, 100-gallon drop fuel

---

*See Hildreth, pp 39-41.

tanks, self-sealing internal fuel tanks, larger wheels and tires, fixed forward-firing nose guns, a simple fixed gunsight, a gun camera, a strike camera, lightweight cockpit armor, and improved communication-navigation gear. The Air Force requested $1.8 million to modify two aircraft to this configuration.[53]

Secretary McNamara approved the plan on 23 March and agreed to allocate the money from the OSD Emergency Fund. The Air Force awarded a contract to the Cessna Aircraft Company on 21 June, and the company delivered the two prototype aircraft six months later, on 12 December 1963.[54]

Pending DOD selection of the YAT-28, YAT-37, or the DDR&E aircraft and its production, the Air Force needed an interim airplane for special warfare operations. The 1st Combat Applications Group evaluated several possibilities during the first few months of 1963 and finally selected the Navy multipurpose A-1E Skyraider as the best possible choice. Thirty miles per hour faster than the T-28, the A-1E carried a one- or two-man crew, had a ferry range of 1,200 miles, and a speed of 265 knots. The aircraft could be converted to any of 12 combat versions, including day or night attack, photoreconnaissance, troop carrier, or ambulance. Another important factor in the selection was that the VNAF had been equipped with the A-1H (a single-seat version) since 1960 and, with USAF assistance, had utilized the aircraft successfully.[55]

On 17 April 1963 the TAC commander personally appealed to the Chief of Staff for priority delivery of the A-1E to improve the scope and rate of operations in South Vietnam. The TAC commander based his appeal on the fact that it was easily maintained, was moderately simple to fly, and was an excellent gun platform. With minor modifications, the A-1E would be capable of carrying all conventional ordnance of the 2,000-pound or smaller class. It had provisions for an assistant pilot or navigator, carried four M-3 20-mm. cannon, and was equipped to carry up to 8,000 pounds of bombs, rockets, torpedoes, mines, and other stores on external racks. For long-range operations, the A-1E could carry auxiliary fuel tanks.[56]

Originally, the Navy had claimed the A-1E was not available but changed its position when faced with the scheduled closing of the Litchfield Park, Ariz., storage area and the need for activating, scrapping, or moving the aircraft to Davis-Monthan AFB, Ariz. Thereupon, the Navy decided in March to make 60 A-1E's and 40 spare engines available to the Air Force.[57]

On 25 April 1963 the Chief of Staff approved an Air Staff recommendation that two A-1E squadrons replace two T-28 special air warfare squadrons. Aircraft modification began in August and was then scheduled at a rate permitting delivery of all A-1E's by December 1964. The work included installation of dual controls and communication-navigation package and a complete overhaul.[58]

* * * * *

The Air Force concluded 1963 with a strengthened special air warfare posture. It had won its fight for a 10-squadron/253-aircraft structure, had formulated and gained approval for its plans to increase special warfare capabilities in SOUTHCOM, EUCOM, and PACOM, and had supported--with some success--STRICOM's requirement for operational control of certain Army-USAF special warfare forces. The Air Force was less successful in its effort to curtail the expansion of organic Army aviation in the special warfare area, and the roles and missions struggle over air support continued unabated.

During 1963 the Air Force adjusted its special warfare forces in accordance with expanding requirements. In the United States, it reorganized SAWC's organizational structure to conform to the growing training and operational mission. In PACAF, the Air Force increased the size of the SAW force and improved command relationships by substituting permanent for TDY units and placing them under the air component commander. To expedite VNAF pilot training, the Air Force inaugurated in-country pilot training. The Air Force arranged to deploy an interim composite squadron to meet USAFE's special warfare needs until the arrival of a permanently assigned unit during fiscal year 1965. In addition, the Air Force increased aid to underdeveloped nations which--although not yet faced with countering active insurgency--were potential trouble spots. Joint Army-USAF civic action and mobile training teams made extended visits to all parts of the free or noncommitted areas of the globe.

The Air Force took concrete action to modernize its SAW aircraft inventory. It approved extensive modification for the B-26 and began testing both a turboprop version of the T-28 and a modified T-37 jet. To provide an interim aircraft until either the improved T-28 or T-37 became available, the Air Force secured 60 Navy A-1E's and was making essential changes to them.

Special air warfare was the concern of the entire Air Force--not only those units specifically designated for the task. SAC's bombers provided the deterrent permitting the use of force at the special warfare level. TAC's Composite Air Strike Forces stood behind the SAW units should the engagement escalate to a higher level of conflict. MATS and TAC troop carrier units were available to furnish additional airlift. Thus, the total strength of the Air Force contributed to the U.S. successes in the field of special warfare.

NOTES

CHAPTER I

1. For documentation of events prior to 1963, see Charles H. Hildreth, USAF Counterinsurgency Doctrines and Capabilities, 1961-1962 (AFCHO, Feb 1964).

2. Chief of Staff Policy Book, 1964, Item 13.

3. AFOS Papers 1/4, 11 Jan 63, subj: USAF Long Range Cold War Objectives.

4. AF Info Policy Ltr for Comdrs, 1 Mar 64.

5. Ltr, CSAF to COMTAC, 3 May 63, subj: CI Force Composition; ASSS by Col A.S. Pouliet of D/Ops, 3 Jul 63, subj: Expansion of USAF SAW Forces, both in Plans RL(63)80-5.

6. JCSM 587-63, 1 Aug 63.

7. Ibid.; USAF PCP 3.39.03.01.4, Jul 63, subj: CI Forces.

8. "White Paper" on General Purpose Forces--Program Package III, nd, pp 25-27, in SW Div files.

9. USAF PCP 3.39.03.01.4.

10. White Paper, p 25.

11. Ibid., p 28; USAF PCP 3.39.03.01.4.

12. USAF PCP 3.39.03.01.4; JCS 1800/739-1, rev 1 Aug 63; Background Paper on USAF Sp Air Warfare, atch to memo, Col A.S. Pouliet to CSAF, 29 Jul 63, subj: Proposed Prog Change--CI Forces (JCS 1800/739-1), in SW Div files; C/S Policy Book, 1964, Item 13-2.

13. Talking Paper on Proposed Prog Change--CI Forces; Talking Paper on Rebuttal to Expected Army Points of Opposition, both atch to memo, Pouliet to CSAF, 29 Jul 63, as cited in n 12; data supplied by SW Div, Jun 64.

14. Talking Paper on Rebuttal, as cited in n 13.

15. JCS 1800/739-1, 29 Jul 63; JCSM 587-63, 1 Aug 63; Prog Change--SOD Decision/Guidance, 30 Oct 63, subj: CI Forces.

16. Briefing prep by SW Div, 20 Sep 62, in SW Div files.

17. Prog Change--Forces, Investment, Operations (Army), 16 Aug 63, subj: Special Forces--CONUS; Background Paper on JCS 1800/749-1, 3 Sep 63, both in Plans RL(63)13.

18. Background Paper, as cited in n 17.

19. Ibid.; interview, author with Col W.V. McBride, Ch/SW Div, 9 Jan 64; atch to ltr, D/Plans, TAC to Hq USAF, 4 Feb 63, subj: Army Unconventional Warfare Doctrine, in SW Div files.

20. Talking Paper on JCS 1800/749-1, 3 Sep 63, in Plans RL(63)13; Background Paper, as cited in n 17.

21. Talking Paper, as cited in n 20.

22. Ibid.; JCS 1800/749-1, rev 17 Sep 63; memo, Chmn/JCS to SOD, 17 Sep 63, subj: PCP Sp Forces, all in Plans RL(63)13.

23. Prog Change--SOD Decision/Guidance, 29 Oct 63, subj: Sp Forces--CONUS; msg 80309, CSAF to USAFSO, 24 Dec 63; intvw with McBride.

24. Memo, SAF to SOD, 12 Dec 63, subj: Organic Aviation for U.S. Army SF; memo, SOD to SAF, 21 Jan 64, same subj, both in OSAF 1960-63.

25. Hildreth, pp 41-43; encl B to JCS 1969/458, 28 Jan 63; JCSM 104-63, 4 Feb 63.

26. Ltr, CINCSTRIKE to JCS, 14 Jan 63, subj: Collocation of Army and AF SW Centers; SACSA 1969/448-1, 21 Jan 63; App A to JCSM 104-63, 4 Feb 63.

27. JCSM 104-63, 4 Feb 63; Background Paper on JCS 1969/458, Jan 63, in Plans RL(63)80-5.

28. App A to JCSM 104-63, 4 Feb 63; SACSA 1969/448-1, 21 Jan 63.

29. App B to JCSM 104-63, 4 Feb 63; Talking Paper on JCS 1969/458, Jan 63, in Plans RL(63)80-5; Staff Study by SW Div, about Nov 63, subj: Orgnzl Structure for SW Joint Ops.

30. Memo, Chmn/JCS to SOD, 13 Feb 63, subj: Collocation of U.S. Army and USAF Activs, in Plans RL(63)80-5.

31. J-5 1969/464/1, 19 Mar 63.

32. Talking Paper on JCS 1969/475, 27 Mar 63, in Plans RL(63)80-5.

33. JCS 1969/475, 29 Mar 63; Staff Study, as cited in n 29.

34. JCSM 258-63, 30 Mar 63; JCS 1969/475, 29 Mar 63.

35. JCS 1259/634-6, 17 Aug 63; JCS 1259/634-12, Sep 63; Hist, D/Plans,

Jul-Dec 63, pp 7, 277-78; Hist, D/Ops, Jul-Dec 63, Sec V, p 5.

36. AF Planners Memo SACSA 20-63, 20 Dec 63, subj: Army and AF SW Forces; memo, Asst Dep D/Plans for Policy to D/Ops, 24 Dec 63, subj: Actions to Improve CI Efforts, both in Plans RL(63)80-5; Hist, D/Plans, Jul-Dec 63, p 278.

37. See sources in n 36.

38. Ltr, D/Plans, TAC to D/Plans, Hq USAF, 4 Feb 63, subj: Army Unconventional Warfare Doctrine; ltr, U.S. Army SW Center to CONARC, 18 Jan 63, subj: Unconventional Warfare; Staff Study, as cited in n 29.

39. Msg STRCC 1469, CINCSTRIKE to Army & AF, 1 Mar 63.

40. Msg DPLW-SA 3-10318, TAC to CSAF, 22 Mar 63; Staff Study, as cited in n 29.

41. Ltr, COMCONARC to CINCSTRIKE, 11 May 63, in SW Div files.

42. Ltr, CINCSTRIKE to COMCONARC, 14 May 63, in SW Div files.

43. Ltr, CINCSTRIKE to COMCONARC, 15 Jun 63, in SW Div files.

44. Ltr, Actg CSA to VCSAF, 25 Jun 63, in SW Div files.

45. Ltr, VCSAF to VCSA, 12 Jul 63, subj: Utilization of Organic Army Aviation in UW Play of Swift Strike III, in SW Div files.

46. Draft rpt by JUWTF-Exercise Swift Strike III, 28 Aug 63, After-Action Report--UW Opnl Joint Exercise Swift Strike III, in SW Div files.

47. M/R by Dep D/Plans for Policy, 24 Oct 63, subj: Meeting of the STRICOM SW Coordinating Gp, in SW Div files.

48. Ibid.

CHAPTER II

1. Hildreth, pp 45-46.

2. Ibid., pp 45-48.

3. TAC SO G-76, 30 Apr 63; Hist, SAWC, Jan-Jun 63, pp 18-22; Hist, TAC, Jan-Jun 63, pp 76-77, Hist, D/Ops, Jul-Dec 63, pp 3-4.

4. TAC SO G-82, 14 May 63; TAC SO G-87, 17 May 63; Hist, SAWC, Jan-Jun 63, pp 21-22.

5. Msg, CINCPAC to JCS, 2 Nov 62; JCS 2343/175, 4 Dec 62; memo, Dep SOD

to Chmn/JCS, 31 Dec 62, subj: Farmgate Augmentation, in OSAF 11-62; Hist, D/Ops, Jan-Jun 63, p 64; Hist, TAC, Jan-Jun 63, p 586.

6. Msgs, CINCPAC to JCS, 23 Jan & 2 Feb 63, both cited in JCS 2343/202, 28 Feb 63; Hist, CINCPAC, 1963, p 213.

7. JCS 2343/202, as amended by SM-318-63, 8 Mar 63; ltr, D/Plans, USAF to VCINCPACAF, 1 Apr 63, subj: Air Augmentation; memo, SOD to Chmn/JCS 26 Mar 63, subj: Air Augmentation, both in Plans RL(63)38-9; Hist, TAC, Jan-Jun 63, p 71.

8. Ltr, D/Plans, USAF to VCINCPACAF, 1 Apr 63, as cited in n 7.

9. AFCCS Ltr 17, 14 Mar 63, subj: USAF Air Effort in Republic of Vietnam; Hist, D/Ops, Jan-Jun 63, pp 64-65, & Jul-Dec 63, Sec V, p 3.

10. CSAFM 188-63, 8 Apr 63; JCS 2343/230, 12 Apr 63.

11. PACAF SO G-44, 3 Jul 63; DAF ltr AFOMO 62n, 17 Jun 63, subj: USAF Air Effort in Republic of Vietnam; AFCCS Ltr 17, 14 Mar 63; Hist, SAWC, Jan-Jun 63, pp 5-6; Hist, D/Ops, Jan-Jun 63, p 64; Hist, D/Ops, Jul-Dec 63, Sec V, pp 2-3.

12. AFCCS Ltr 17, 14 Mar 63; MJCS 34-64, 2 Mar 64, subj: Dev Status of Mil CI Progs, Incl CI Forces, Sec III, p 85; Hist, TAC, Jan-Jun 63, pp 597-98.

13. MJCS 34-64, 2 Mar 64, Sec III, p 34; Hist, D/Ops, Jul-Dec, Sec III, p 1.

14. Memo, VCSAF to SAF, 7 Mar 63, subj: Aircraft and Pilots for the VNAF, in OSAF 290-63.

15. Transcript of meeting at Gia Palace, 17 Dec 62, between President of SVN, SAF, U.S. Ambassador, Comdr 2d Air Div, & DCS/P&O for PACAF, in OSAF 290-63.

16. JCS 2343/224, 25 Apr 63.

17. Memo, SOD to SAF, 27 May 63, subj: Aircraft and Pilots for the VNAF; proposed news release, Aug 63, subj: Viet Nam Cessna 185 Training Prog, both in OSAF 290-63; msg 3288-63, PACAF to CINCPAC, 19 Jun 63, in Plans RL(63)38-5-2; Sups to Hq USAF Daily Staff Digest 31 & 34, 14 Jun & 12 Jul 63; Hist, CINCPAC, 1963, p 211.

18. Msg 3259-63, PACAF to CSAF, 10 May 63; msg 0800 382, CINCPAC to CSAF, 8 May 63; msg 3288-63 & Sups to Staff Digest, as cited in n 17; Hist, CINCPAC, 1963, p 210.

19. Hist, CINCPAC, 1963, p 211.

20. Msg OPLS 84081, USAFE to CSAF, 7 Jun 63; msg ECJC-S 10358, USCINCEUR

Notes to pages 36-46   61

to JCS, 11 Jun 63; memo, CSAF to Chmn/JCS, 20 Jul 63, subj: Rpt to the Pres on Utilization of SF Units, all in Plans RL(63)80-5; memo, Dep D/Plans for Policy to D/Ops, 25 Jun 63, subj: Actions to Improve CI Efforts, in SW Div files.

21. Memo, CSAF to Chmn/JCS, 20 Jul 63, as cited in n 20.

22. MJCS 148-63, 18 Sep 63, subj: Dev Status of Mil CI Progs, Incl Counterguerrilla Forces as of 1 Aug 63; msg CINC 404, USAFE to CSAF, 3 Dec 63, in Plans RL(63)80-5.

23. Msg 80997, CSAF to USAFE, 28 Dec 63.

24. Ibid.; JCS 2147/307-1, 26 Dec 63; Hist, D/Plans, Jul-Dec 63, pp 274-75.

25. Memo, Ch/SW Div to D/Plans, 12 Jun 63, subj: Increased COIN Forces in Panama, in SW Div files; MJCS 34-64, 2 Mar 64, Sec III, p 34; DAF ltr AFOMO 107m, 24 Oct 63, subj: Activation of 605th Air Commando Sq, Comp & . . . Actions; Hist, D/Ops, Jul-Dec 63, pp 3-4.

26. Address by Gen C.E. LeMay, CSAF, before Central States Shrine Asso, St. Louis, Mo., 19 Oct 63.

27. 1st ind to ltr, D/M&O to SW Div, 19 Feb 63, subj: AF Objectives in the Civic Actions Prog, in Plans RL(63)80-5.

28. Sup 132 to AF Policy Ltr for Comdrs, Jun 64, pp 18, 23.

29. C/S Policy Book, 1964, Item 13-3; Hist, CAIRC, Jan-Jun 63, pp 239-40.

30. Hist, CAIRC, Jan-Jun 63, pp 288, 364-65.

31. Msg C-17-62-C, USAFSO to CSAF, 11 Oct 63; M/R by Lt Col D.M. Clark, SW Div, 21 Aug 63, in Plans RL(63)80-4; Sup 132 to AF Policy Ltr for Comdrs, Jun 64, pp 12-13.

32. Msg C-17-62-C, as cited in n 31; Hist, TAC, Jan-Jun 63, pp 435-36.

33. Hist, CAIRC, Jan-Jun 63, pp 318-19.

34. Ibid., pp 425-27.

35. Ibid., pp 349-50, 385.

36. Ibid., pp 288, 425-27.

37. Msg 10050, CAIRC to CSAF, 28 Mar 63; Hist, CAIRC, Jan-Jun 63, pp 208, 287-89, 339, 427; Hist, D/Ops, Jan-Jun 63, p 66.

38. Msg OPL-C 10099, CAIRC to CSAF, 8 Jun 63.

39. Hist, SAWC, Jan-Jun 63, pp 139-40; Hist, D/Ops, Jan-Jun 63, p 65.

40. Msg 89100, SAF to TAC, 29 Mar 63; memo, Dep D/Plans for Policy to D/Ops, 29 Feb 63, subj: Actions to Improve USAF CI Efforts; Hist, SAWC, Jan-Jun 63, pp 142-43; Hist, D/Ops, Jan-Jun 63, p 65.

41. Hist, SAWC, Jan-Jun 63, pp 141-42.

42. Atch to Talking Paper on PCP--Counterinsurgency Forces, Jul 63, in SW Div files.

43. Msg DORF-FT 3 11021, TAC to CSAF, 20 Jun 63.

44. Ibid.; ltr, D/Plans, USAF to TAC, 26 Aug 63, subj: Estb of Mil Tng Teams for Worldwide Ops, in Plans RL(63)80-5; Hist, D/Plans, Jul-Dec 63, p 286.

45. Memo, President to SOD, 15 Jul 63, in Plans RL(63)80-5.

46. Msg 79247, CSAF to USAFE, PACAF, USAFSO, 16 Jul 63; M/R by Col W.P. Anderson, SW Div, 10 Sep 63, in Plans RL(63)80-5; app to Encl A, JCS 1969/490/1, 22 Jul 63.

47. M/R by Anderson, as cited in n 46; msg 84061, CSAF to USAFE, PACAF, USAFSO, 2 Aug 63.

48. Memo, President to Sec/State, 26 Jul 63; Sum of JCS Joint CI Conf, 30-31 Jul 63, 26 Aug 63, Agenda Item 6, both in OSAF 116-63; Circular Airgram 1507, State-AID-DOD to Ambassadors, 6 Aug 63, in Plans RL(63)80-5.

49. Intvw with McBride, 9 Jan 64; memo, Asst Dep D/Plans for Policy to Asst/Mut Scty, 20 Dec 63, subj: Joint DOD-AID-State Airgrams Concerning SF & MTT's; memo, Asst Dep D/Plans for Policy to D/Ops, 24 Dec 63, subj: Actions to Improve CI Efforts, both in Plans RL(63)80-5.

50. Memo, Dep D/Aero Progs to SW Div, 14 May 63, subj: Actions to Improve COIN Efforts; ltr, CSAF to COMTAC, 3 May 63, subj: COIN Force Composition; AFCSS Ltr 29, 25 Apr 63, subj: Strike Aircraft for USAF Sp Forces, all three in Plans RL(63)80-5; Hist, D/Ops, Jan-Jun 63, p 67, & Jul-Dec 63, Sec V, p 4; Hist, TAC, Jan-Jun 63, pp 415-18.

51. Hist, D/Opnl Rqmts, Jan-Jun 63, pp 79, 122-23.

52. AFCSS Ltr 29, 25 Apr 63; ltr, CSAF to TAC, 3 May 63; Hist, D/Opnl Rqmts, Jul-Dec 63, p 80; Hist, TAC, Jan-Jun 63, pp 425-27.

53. Memo, SAF to DDR&E, 1 Feb 63, subj: CI Aircraft Dev; ASSS by Lt Col L.H. Batsel of D/Opnl Rqmts, 24 Jan 63, same subj, both in OSAF 495-62; Hist, TAC, Jan-Jun 63, pp 78-79.

54. Memo, DDR&E to SAF, 6 May 63, subj: FY 1963 Emerg Fund Transfer for CI Aircraft Dev; ASSS by Ch/Tac Div, D/Dev, 13 Jun 63; memo, U-Secy/AF to DDR&E, 19 Jun 63, all same subj, all three in OSAF 116-63; Hist, D/Opnl Rqmts, Jul-Dec 63, p 80; USAF Current Status Rpt, Jan 64, Sec II, p 32.

Notes to pages 53-54

55. Hist, SAWC, Jan-Jun 63, p 4; 1st ind (AFCHO to D/Plans, 11 Jun 64, subj: AFCHO Historical Study), SW Div to AFCHO, 19 Jun 64.

56. Ltr, COMTAC to CSAF, 17 Apr 63, as cited in Hist, TAC, Jan-Jun 63, p 420.

57. Msg C-3016, TAC to USAF, 20 Feb 63; TAC Daily Diary, 11 Mar 63, both as cited in Hist, TAC, Jan-Jun 63, pp 441-42.

58. AFCSS Ltr 29, 25 Apr 63; USAF Current Status Rpt, Jan 64, Sec II, p 32; Hist, SAWC, Jan-Jun 63, p 4; Hist, D/Opnl Rqmts, Jan-Jun 63, p 79; Hist, D/Ops, Jul-Dec 63, Sec V, pp 4-5.

GLOSSARY

ACG	Air Commando Group
AFOB	Air Force Operating Base
AFOS	Air Force Objectives Series
AID	Agency for International Development
ASSS	Air Staff Summary Sheet
ATC	Air Training Command
CAIRC	Caribbean Air Command
CARIBCOM	Caribbean Command
CCTS	Combat Crew Training Squadron
CI	Counterinsurgency
CINCLANT	Commander in Chief Atlantic
CINCNELM	Commander in Chief U.S. Naval Forces Eastern Atlantic and Mediterranean
COIN	Counterinsurgency
CONARC	Continental Army Command
CSA	Chief of Staff Army
CSAF	Chief of Staff Air Force
DDR&E	Director of Defense Research and Engineering
FTD	Field Training Detachment
JSCP	Joint Strategic Capabilities Plan
JSOP	Joint Strategic Objectives Plan
JSWCG	Joint Special Warfare Coordinating Group
JUWOB	Joint Unconventional Warfare Operating Base
JUWTF	Joint Unconventional Warfare Task Force
MAAG	Military Assistance Advisory Group
MACV	Military Assistance Command Vietnam
MAP	Military Assistance Program
MEAFSA	Middle East, Africa South of the Sahara, and Southern Asia
M/R	Memo for Record
MTT	Mobile Training Team
OSD	Office, Secretary of Defense
PCP	Program Change Proposal
SACSA	Special Assistant for Counterinsurgency and Special Activities
SAW	Special Air Warfare
SAWC	Special Air Warfare Center
SF	Special Forces
SFOB	Special Forces Operating Base
STRICOM	Strike Command
SVN	South Vietnam
SW	Special Warfare
USAFSO	U.S. Air Forces Southern Command
USSOUTHCOM	U.S. Southern Command
UW	Unconventional Warfare
VNAF	Vietnamese Air Force

DISTRIBUTION

HQ USAF

1.	SAF-OS	54.	AFSDC		
2.	SAF-US	55.	AFSLP		
3.	SAF-RR	56.	AFSMS		
4.	SAF-AA	57.	AFSME		
5.	SAF-LL	58.	AFSPP		
6-10.	SAF-OI	59.	AFSPD		
11.	SAF-MP	60.	AFSSS		
12.	SAF-FM	61.	AFSTP		
13.	SAF-RD	62.	AFSDC		
14.	SAF-IL	63-65.	AFXOP		
15.	AFCVC	66-68.	AFXPD		
16.	AFBSA	69.	AFTAC		
17.	AFDAS				
18.	AFESS				

MAJOR COMMANDS

70.	ACIC
71.	ADC
72-73.	AFCS
74.	AFLC
75-79.	AFSC
80-81.	ATC
82-83.	AU
84.	AFAFC
85.	AAC
86.	USAFSO
87-88.	CONAC
89.	HEDCOM
90-94.	MATS
95.	OAR
96-100.	PACAF
101-107.	SAC
108-112.	TAC
113.	USAFA
114-118.	USAFE
119-121.	USAFSS

HQ USAF (continued):

19. AFFRA
20. AFGOA
21-25. AFIIS
26. AFJAG
27. AFMSG
28. AFNIN
29. AFAAC
30. AFAAF
31. AFABF
32. AFADA
33. AFADS
34. AFAMA
35. AFAUD
36. AFODC
37. AFOAP
38. AFOCC
39. AFOCE
40. AFOMO
41. AFORQ
42. AFPDC
43. AFPCP
44. AFPDP
45. AFPDS
46. AFPMP
47. AFPTR
48. AFRDC
49. AFRDD
50. AFRDP
51. AFRNE
52. AFRRP
53. AFRST

OTHER

122-123.	ASI
124-128.	ASI (HAF)
129-133.	ASI (HA)
134-200.	AFCHO (Stock)

www.ingramcontent.com/pod-product-compliance
Lightning Source LLC
Chambersburg PA
CBHW050504110426
42742CB00018B/3368